EDMUND
THORNTON
JENKINS

Edmund Thornton Jenkins, ca. 1913. *Courtesy the late Edwina Fleming of Charleston, S.C.*

EDMUND THORNTON JENKINS

The Life and Times of an
American Black Composer,
1894-1926

JEFFREY P. GREEN

CONTRIBUTIONS TO THE STUDY OF
MUSIC AND DANCE, NUMBER 2

GREENWOOD PRESS
WESTPORT, CONNECTICUT • LONDON, ENGLAND

Library of Congress Cataloging in Publication Data

Green, Jeffrey P.
    Edmund Thornton Jenkins.

    (Contributions to the study of music and dance,
ISSN 0193-9041; no. 2)
    Bibliography: p.
    Includes index.
    1. Jenkins, Edmund Thornton, 1894–   . 2. Com-
posers—United States—Biography. I. Title. II. Series.
ML410.J44G7   780'.92'4 [B]   81-23721
ISBN 0-313-23253-9 (lib. bdg.)   AACR2

Library of Congress Catalog Card Number: 81-23721
ISBN: 0-313-23253-9
ISSN: 0193-9041

First published in 1982

Greenwood Press
A division of Congressional Information Service, Inc.
88 Post Road West, Westport, Connecticut 06881

Printed in the United States of America

10 9 8 7 6 5 4 3 2 1

Copyright Acknowledgments

The author and publisher are grateful for permission
to reprint from the following works.

Peter J. Pirie, *The English Musical Renaissance* (London:
Victor Gollancz Ltd, 1979).
Colin Scott-Sutherland, *Arnold Bax* (London: J M Dent & Sons
Ltd Publishers, 1973).
Personal letters to Jenkins from Randall H. Lockhart.
The Crisis Magazine, New York, November 1926.

Every reasonable effort has been made to trace the owners of copyright materials in
this book, but in some instances this has proven impossible. The publishers will be
glad to receive information leading to more complete acknowledgments in
subsequent printings of the book, and in the meantime extend their apologies for
any omissions.

To Edwina Fleming of Charleston, South Carolina,
and John Chilton of London, England, whose humor,
trust, and cooperation made this work possible; and
to Rainer Lotz of Bonn, Germany, and my brother,
who encouraged my interest in black music—
and also for Maureen.

CONTENTS

ILLUSTRATIONS

ACKNOWLEDGMENTS

This work would not have been possible without the guidance and assistance of the following.

Belgium: Robert Pernet

Canada: Claude Vigneron

Caribbean: The Advocate (Barbados); Herman D. Boxill (Antigua); Felix "Harry" Leekam (Trinidad); Randall H. Lockhart (Dominica); Tony Martin (Trinidad); H. L. Wynter of *The Daily Gleaner* (Jamaica).

England: Frank Alcindor; Bruce Bastin; Mark Berresford; Clyde Binfield; John Chilton; Jim Connor; David Cull; Chris Ellis; Ken Fidgen; Laura Gilbert; Doris Hare; Gerald Howat; Amy Barbour-James; Ron Jewson; Don Knight; Jan-Erik Knutsen; Vivian Langrish; Mimi Leekam; Bert Lemon; Dennis Plowright; Betty Purcell; R. N. G. Rowland; Brian Rust; Eva Sharpe; Alyn Shipton; Winifred Small; Avril Coleridge-Taylor; Leslie Thompson; Edward S. Walker; Brian Willan; Dr. Barnardo's Homes; the British Library; University of Cambridge Archives; the General Medical Council; Guildhall Library (Ian Rivers); Imperial War Museum; Hon. Soc. of the Inner Temple; Metropolitan Tabernacle; Müller Homes for Children; Pharmaceutical Society of Great Britain; Public Record Office; Queen's College, Taunton; Rhodes House Library; Royal Academy of Music (Luisa Berra, Jane Harington, Robin Golding); Royal College of Music; Royal College of Organists; Royal Commonwealth Society (D. H. Simpson); St. Catharine's College, Cambridge; Spurgeon's College; the Consulate-General of France; the

U.S. Embassy; and the librarians in the London Boroughs of Bromley, Croydon, Ealing, Islington, Wandsworth and Westminster; R. A. Bowden, Archivist, Marylebone Library, and the staff at West Sussex libraries in Crawley and Worthing.

France: Arthur Briggs; Bertrand Demeusy; Pierre Gazères; Fabrice Weill; Jacques Weill; Hôpital Tenon; SACEM (Patrick Briel).

Germany: Imanuel Geiss; Franz Hoffmann; Rainer Lotz; Karl Gert zur Heide.

Netherlands: Dr. Jazz magazine

Scotland: George Shepperson; University of Edinburgh library

Sweden: Sonia Huhn

United States of America: In Charleston: Francis Brenner; Margaretta P. Childs; Arthur Clement, Jr.; Holland W. Daniels; John E. Dowling; Sarah Dowling; Frances Edmunds; Edwina Fleming; Lucius Goggins; Lonnie Hamilton III; Eugene Hunt; Robert Mills; Sara Nicholls; Inez Nimmons; Emma Reed; George Shepherd; Joseph Simmons; Rebecca Stepney; Thomas R. Waring; André Woods; Thelma Woods; Ashley Hall school; Charleston Museum; Dart Hall Library; Jenkins Orphanage; *News and Courier;* South Carolina Historical Society.

Elsewhere in the United States: Miriam Brown; Olive Campbell; Samuel Floyd, Jr.; Dick Hadlock; Alfred Haughton; Robert A. Hill; Clifton H. Johnson; Tony Martin; Eileen Southern; Martha Stiles; Jane Wells; Wendell Whalum; Amos White; Library of Congress; New York Public Libraries; Passport Office.

Wales: Derwyn Jones; Ivor Wynne Jones; Alex Munro; University College of North Wales, Bangor.

My thanks to them and the many others who have helped. To Randall Lockhart I owe a special debt which I hope is evidenced by this study of his friend. The errors are mine.

EDMUND THORNTON JENKINS

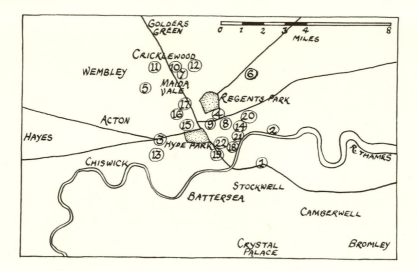

1) Spurgeon's Tabernacle
2) Sir George Williams's offices, St. Paul's
    Churchyard
3) The White City exhibition and stadium,
    Shepherd's Bush
4) Royal Academy of Music and Duke's Hall,
    York Gate
5) Brondesbury Park
6) Marlborough Theater
7) Sumatra Road
8) Queen's Hall, Langham Place
9) Wigmore Hall, Wigmore Street
10) Westbere Road
11) Pine Road
12) Goldhurst Terrace
13) The *Palais de Danse*, Hammersmith
14) Bloomsbury Street
15) St. Mary's Hospital
16) Paddington Infirmary
17) Lauderdale Mansions
18) Central Hall, Westminster
19) Denison House, Vauxhall Bridge Road, Victoria
20) Doughty Street
21) Savoy Theater and Savoy Hotel
22) Buckingham Palace

1. Sketch map of London, *drawn by Mary Knutsen.*

CHAPTER 1

THE OSTRACISED, SUPPRESSED, AND DEPRESSED

The Britons who colonized South Carolina in the late seventeenth century named the province after their king, Charles II. Their settlement of Charleston was on a low peninsula between two broad rivers, the Ashley and the Cooper, named in honor of one of the original lords proprietors, Sir Anthony Ashley Cooper, later the first Lord Shaftesbury. The colony grew as rice, indigo, and, later, cotton plantations were established in the swamp country inland and on the sea islands along the coast. The first African slaves were imported from the Caribbean soon after Charleston was founded, and they soon outnumbered the European population. Black and white links with the West Indies continued as the town grew to become North America's fourth most populated city. French and Spanish refugees settled in the city after the black uprising of 1791 in Haiti, and the cosmopolitan atmosphere of Charleston was encouraged by its trade with Europe, Africa, the Caribbean, and other American settlements, and by the wealthy merchants and planters who sent their children to be educated in Britain and France. Charleston had an active theater, a city college, the oldest music society in North America (the Saint Cecilia), and an impressive list of "firsts": America's first railway; the first naval success in the War of Independence against Britain; the first museum in the Western Hemisphere; and the first shot in the American Civil War, when Fort Sumter in the sea approaches to Charleston harbor was bombarded.

The city and the surrounding country had survived wars with the Indians and threats from disease, hurricanes, flood, fire, and earthquake. It had defended itself against attacks from pirates, the French, the Spanish, and the British, and slave unrest and rebellion. South Carolina's secession from the Union in 1860 and the subsequent bombardment of Fort Sumter led to years of warfare and a long seige of Charleston, ended by occupation by federal troops, the imposition of rule from Washington, and the freeing of the slaves. Plantations were destroyed by occupying Northern troops, and the economy of the city and state was in ruins.

People sympathetic to the plight of the freed slaves worked to establish schools and other institutions to assist the mass of illiterate peasants. A sizeable minority of South Carolina's black population had been neither plantation workers nor whiteowned, having obtained a measure of freedom, by purchase or gift, classifying them as Free Persons of Color. Active as barbers, carpenters, or tailors, or in other relatively independent occupations, they owned property, paid taxes, and, before emancipation, had even owned slaves. Members of this literate and socially organized group were the natural leaders of the now free black people of South Carolina, although their position as upper-caste blacks had been somewhat unhappy. They had been free enough to emigrate to west Africa, but often such liberty had been obtained from their masters on the condition that they went to the American Colonization Society colony of Liberia.

In the postwar chaos of South Carolina, Daniel Joseph Jenkins, born in slavery 100 miles from Charleston, became a leader of his people. He was respected by Charleston whites and blacks, active in church and civic affairs, a minister of the Baptist church, the founder and editor of a weekly newspaper that appeared for over forty years, the president of the only orphanage for black children in South Carolina, and the father of Edmund Thornton Jenkins, Associate of the Royal Academy of Music (London), composer and multiinstrumentalist.

Daniel Jenkins was born in June 1862,[1] in either Bamberg or Barnwell County,[2] S.C. He had none of the advantages of the Free Persons of Color. He recalled his childhood thus: "When I was a boy I was put to work and given six quarts of meal, two pounds of meat and a quart of molasses a week and I lived on it for a year."[3]

An orphanage publication stated, "He was brought up in the house of Mrs. J. D. Dickerson, of Bamberg, S.C. His mother was an earnest worker, and much success is no doubt due to her counsel, together with Mr. and Mrs. J. D. Dickerson—she was a woman of simple and earnest life, but unremitting toil. Thus it can be easily seen where the son inherited his peculiar naturalness of mind, that charming simplicity of character, which is always admired by those who meet him."[4]

In common with many black Americans after the abolition of slavery Jenkins had abandoned the name given by white authority. His original name is reported as Curtis, Kirklands, Stricklands, Dickson, and Dickerson.[5] His reasons for selecting Jenkins are obscure, although it is not an uncommon name in South Carolina. It is probable that Daniel's names were in honor of Joseph Jenkins Roberts, the Virginia-born black who was the first president of the African Republic of Liberia, one of the few countries where blacks were in power. The United States recogized Liberia's nationhood in the year of Daniel's birth, which was also when Roberts took a well-publicized tour of Europe, where Liberia's independence had been acknowledged in 1847.

Liberia was of continuing interest to blacks in America; interest in west Africa as a whole grew among South Carolina blacks beginning in 1876. Resident in Charleston from 1870 was Martin R. Delany, who had traveled in Nigeria in 1859–1960 with Robert Campbell, a Jamaican.[6] Delany had worked with the freed slaves at Hilton Head and Saint Helena Island, South Carolina, from 1865, and published four pamphlets on aspects of black rights in Charleston, where he had become one of the blacks in high executive office. He established *The Charleston Independent* in 1875 and was involved in local politics. Following the withdrawal of federal troops from South Carolina in April 1877 many blacks felt that their economic and political future in the United States was bleak, and turned to the solution proposed by Delany and the English African Aid Society in 1860, which was settlement outside the United States.

Celebrations of the thirtieth anniversary of Liberia's declaration of independence, when four thousand blacks paraded through Charleston in July 1877, led to thousands of Carolina blacks registering with the Rev. B. F. Porter's "Liberia Exodus Association."

Monies were collected, a joint stock company formed, and a ship was purchased. Renamed the *Azor* in Charleston in March 1878, this black *Mayflower* carried a group of hopeful black emigrants to Africa. Edmund Jenkins was to have connections with Liberia, which has been described as "a little bit of South Caroline, of Georgia, of Virginia—that is to say—of the ostracised, suppressed, depressed, elements of those States—tacked on to West Africa."[7]

The *Azor* scheme collapsed after a series of unfortunate incidents: polluted water was responsible for the death of over twenty passengers and necessitated an unscheduled stop at Freetown, Sierra Leone; the return voyage carried neither passengers nor freight; the captain sued the company and the ship was impounded; the enthusiasm to leave the United States had left three hundred ex-slaves in Charleston and the company looked after them, which was a severe strain on its limited resources; and the *Azor* had to be used for coastal trade in order to pay off debts, which, under the guidance of Delany and his son, was done by the middle of 1880. Blacks had lost confidence in the company, which passed into obscurity, although its legacy was the missionary efforts of the African Methodist Episcopal Church, which first ventured to Africa on the *Azor* and is still active in Africa one hundred years later.

Daniel Jenkins, along with many Carolina blacks after the collapse of the emigration scheme, traveled west to Arkansas,[8] probably after September 1881, when he married the sixteen-year-old South Carolina-born Lena James.[9] Severe discontent was widespread among South Carolina blacks at this time, for the promises of the immediate post–Civil War period had not materialized and the mass of black peasantry still owned no land. The land tenure systems of the whites were rejected by so many blacks, who left the land for Charleston, Africa, or the west, that the state legislated against emigration in 1880. Thousands of blacks were reported in Augusta, Georgia, in late December 1881, awaiting the arrival of their special train to carry them to Arkansas. Augusta is not far from Barnwell County and Bamberg where the land tenure system was very unpopular. Jenkins and his September bride were probably part of this exodus.

Daniel Jenkins's early years were described in a newspaper report, published six years after his death, which said that he had operated a store and a farm successfully for several years, moved to Arkansas, and returned to South Carolina to reside at Ladson, later moving seventeen miles to Charleston, where he went into the wood business.[11] Jenkins is reported as having been active by 1885 in church work at Five Mile Station, on Charleston Neck, between the city and Ladson, by which time he had a growing family.[12]

There were to be eleven children, apparently including two twin births. Stirling Herbert Jenkins was the oldest boy. His brothers were Joseph, Hawthorne, Howard, Edward, Nathaniel, and Edmund. The four girls were Esther, Lena, Roxie, and Mildred. Only Mildred lived to see old age, passing in 1981.

Life in South Carolina in the mid-1880s was tough for Daniel and Lena Jenkins and their family, but the blatant racism of later years had yet to develop. Thomas McCants Stewart, a twenty-nine-year-old black Charleston-born lawyer and journalist, reported for a northern journal on his trip through South Carolina in 1885, writing from Columbia, the state capital, in April 1885 "I feel about as safe here as in Providence, R.I. I can ride in the first-class cars on the railroads and in the streets. I can go into saloons and get refreshments even as in New York."[13]

Daniel Jenkins is reported to have attended Benedict College, which had been founded as Benedict Institute in 1871, and was an important black Baptist training school. Interviews with those who knew him, albeit in his later life, failed to confirm reports that he had studied theology there from 1889.[14] Surviving friends doubted that he had attended school for more than a few months, and certainly no more than two years.

In 1891 the state passed further legislation to discourage easy emigration by blacks. The economy was based on a mass of peasant black labor with few land rights to grow primary produce, mainly cotton, on white labor in mills and processing plants, and on white merchants and traders fixing prices, credit, and supplies. The leadership of the black community was still mainly in the hands of the Free People of Color (often of mixed race) with some influence levied by blacks from the exslave population. Black leaders had failed to wrest political control from the whites and had also been made less effective by corruption and incompetence.[15] The churches continued to be an important influence in the black community, providing meeting places for social, political, and religious events, allowing leaders to emerge through personal strength, and encouraging literacy, charity, community work, and self-help.

Daniel Jenkins's concern for the more unfortunate blacks of South Carolina took up a great deal of his time and money by 1891. His timber business often took him to Charleston, and one December he befriended some homeless waifs who had sought shelter in a freight car. Thereafter Jenkins continued the responsibility of looking after homeless black waifs and urchins who roamed the city, supporting his efforts with assistance from his church and friends throughout 1891.

> He soon saw that his limited funds as a colored pastor would not allow him to carry on as he wished with the work that was near and dear to his heart. He did not like to beg, not even for the little motherless and fatherless boys and girls who looked to him for food, clothing, an education and the things that go to make up a happy, well-rounded life.[16]

In July 1892 Jenkins formally incorporated the Orphan Aid Society and committed himself to a life of social work that was to make his name known throughout black America.

The Orphan Aid Society was soon known as the Jenkins Orphanage, but, like its founder, its origins are somewhat obscure. It started in a building in northern Charleston, at 660 King Street, described as "an old shed" in one of the tracts issued by the orphanage to obtain support and donations. Another tract says that the hundred or so stray children moved to a building at 20 Franklin Street, in downtown Charleston, in 1892. Something of Daniel Jenkin's character, influence, and contacts may be seen in the fact that the orphans were allowed to occupy such a substantial building, which was described in the same tract: "This building can accommodate more boys than we can get means to support. This is among the largest buildings in Charleston, being a three-storied brick structure, and one of the landmarks of this old historic city."[17]

The Old Marine Hospital at 20 Franklin Street had been designed by Charleston architect Robert Mills and built in 1833. It had been a hospital during the seige, and after 1865 it was a free school for black children, run by local white women. A sign of the deterioration in the city's fortunes was that such a building was available to Jenkins, although another Mills building, the city jail, adjoined the hospital's northern wall, and the area did not have prime property values. Executions were carried out a few feet from the orphanage wall until July 1911.

In October 1892 Jenkins became the pastor of the Fourth Baptist Church on Palmetto Street. He arranged a new building at a cost of over five thousand dollars, an indication of his fund-raising abilities. The orphanage paid a nominal rent for the Franklin Street premises and was entitled to renew the five-year lease "on condition that it is kept in repair, the taxes and insurance paid, and that the school is properly and successfully conducted."[18] This 1893 document states that twenty of the children were being fed and clothed by the society, whose responsibilities extended to the general education of a total of three hundred children. "A corps of colored teachers takes charge of this large number, and proper rules and regulations are observed. The children belong to a class much in need and worthy of help, and the Orphanage, it is hoped, will save many from ignorance and vice."

Prominent white citizens supported Jenkins's efforts. His advisory board in 1893 were: John F. Ficken (the mayor); George W. Williams (president of the Carolina Savings Bank); Dr. Francis L. Parker (dean of the medical college); Frank R. Frost (an attorney); and William G. Harvey, Jr. (superintendent of the Bradstreet Agency). They assured the charitable that donations would be honestly and judiciously expended under their supervision. Another white citizen who gave valuable help to the orphanage was Dr. Edward F. Parker, who operated a free dispensary for the treatment of diseases of the eye, ear, and throat on the Franklin Street premises.

Jenkins did not rely solely on the support of local sympathizers. He made continuous efforts to obtain donations from outside the Carolinas. "Taking a leaf from Booker T. Washington, who successfully raised money through his Tuskegee Singers, Daniel Jenkins began early to exploit small Negroes playing band music. He obtained some battered horns, organized a band which he sent North in 1893 to play on street corners."[19] "During the time the children were not in school [the band] would make tours of the United States, performing in cities and towns and bringing into the treasury of the Orphanage funds for its support. The boys in the band became a means of honorable income for the institution."[20]

Black institutions other than Tuskegee had used music to obtain funds, perhaps the most famous being Fisk University, whose Jubilee Singers traveled to Europe in the 1870s.[21] Vocal groups were part of the orphanage's musical activities, but from the earliest days of the enterprise there were brass bands at the Jenkins Orphanage.

By the end of 1893 Parson Jenkins was responsible for 360 children, his own family, the Palmetto Street church, and the installments on a printing press that he had obtained from Damon and Peets in New York.[22] The orphanage arranged a fair in February 1894, with a fourteen-piece brass band and other entertainments for Charleston's black community.[23] The poster was printed in New York, indicating that the press was not yet functioning.

On April 9, 1894, probably at the family home at 20 Franklin Street, Mrs. Lena Jenkins gave birth to another boy, to be named Edmund Thornton Jenkins. His middle name was in recognition of Miss E. A. Thornton of Washington, D.C., who helped at the orphanage at this time. One of the male supporters of Jenkins in his daily work was Paul Daniels, a short black man, who was about twenty-three years old. The Daniels family was involved with the orphanage as much as the Jenkins family, and the families may have been related. To avoid confusion, Daniel Joseph Jenkins was called "Uncle Joseph" by close friends, and "Parson Jenkins" by the orphans and adults.

In June 1894 George Williams requested that Mr. H. W. Hubbard, the treasurer of the American Missionary Association, 56 Read Street, New York, arrange a donation to the orphanage from the Daniel Hand Educational Fund for Colored People. Williams told Hubbard that the orphanage had "nearly five hundred Negro boys and girls, little waifs picked up in the streets and by-ways."[24] Further white support is evidenced in the same tract, which quotes a letter of July 2, 1894, from former state Senator Augustine T. Smythe, a lawyer and merchant of Charleston who had reached the rank of major in the Confederate army after he escaped from Charleston at the end of the war.

On October 13, 1894, the Jenkins Orphanage printing press issued the first copy of *The Charleston Messenger*.[25] The weekly newspaper gave vocational training to the small boys in the orphanage and promoted the orphanage, as well as employing adult blacks who were unable to work for white-owned papers. Only two editions from before 1935 have been traced.

The brass bands were the largest single source of revenue for the orphanage; they were to have a great deal of influence in America, as the child musicians left Charleston each summer, taking their music to other cities. No former Orphanage musician recalls playing west of Chicago, but they traveled great distances each year. In 1895 the band crossed the Atlantic to gather funds and support in England. Parson Jenkins made many contacts during these months abroad, as did Paul Daniels, who seems to have remained in Britain for four years.

CHAPTER 2

THE IMPECUNIOUS REPRESENTATIVES

In a tract to solicit alms and assistance, published by 1913, Parson Jenkins described why he had taken the brass band to England in 1895.

> In 1895, after the big storm, our Orphanage building was wrecked and we got in a debt of $1,700. I took 18 of the orphans North, to play and give entertainments, all being green, we scarcely made our expenses. Just about the time we started back home, and the big debt loomed up before me. I felt that I had rather die than to return to Charleston without the money to cancel the debt. Some good white friends met me while in a spirit of despondency, and advised me to go over to England, saying that I would get barrels of money and I imagined on hearing them that I could just see the money bubbling up before me. Nothing doubting, neither counting up the cost, I leaped out without a dollar only had half enough to pay our way, but the captain took us over any way, expecting to make money on the ship, but in less than a half hour's time after getting on the ship we became seasick and remained so until the day before we landed.

This trip to England was probably an ambitious extension of the usual summer travels, encouraged by hurricane damage, and the terms of the lease which had run for much of its initial five years.

There are reasons to consider that Parson Jenkins had been in Britain before 1895, but his knowledge of British ways was not enough to save him from being arrested in London. Orphanage tracts avoid this aspect of the adventure, merely hinting at the problem

> I took the boys out to play on the streets, but their strange appearance created so much excitement and monopolized the thoroughfares to such an extent that we at once were forced to retire, also under the English law, boys at the age of ours were forbidden to play instruments.[1]

Parson Jenkins was tried at Bow Street Magistrates Court at the beginning of September 1895 on a charge of exploiting child labor. Following recent political agitation by the late Lord Shaftesbury, the descendant of one of the founders of Charleston, children under the age of eleven could not be employed in England. This was not the only London link with Charleston, for Augustine Smythe and his family were in London. "Since he did a great deal of the law business for Jenkins Orphanage the whole family was very familiar with the bands and their 'music' from the youngest beginners, who stayed at home, through the eldest who traveled. Therefore when they heard the unmistakeable nostalgic strains coming round the London corner they definitely perked up their ears."[2] Smythe helped the distressed black youngsters.

The court case was reported in detail in London's *The Daily Telegraph* of September 9, 1895, "The other day, the Rev. D. J. Jenkins, a Baptist minister of colour, and of Charlestown, America, entered the Bow Street Police Court, followed by thirteen little negro boys of ages ranging from five to fourteen, and informed the sitting magistrate that he had come over to this country to raise funds for an orphanage with which he was connected in Charlestown." The lengthy report has a labored humor, and comments "Much may be done, no doubt, to raise money for an orphanage, but to let loose a brass band of thirteen negro children upon an urban population suffering with nerves is likely to create almost as many orphans as it would relieve."

The magistrate gave one sovereign (£1, or $5) to assist Jenkins and his band return to the United States, but Parson Jenkins did not leave England immediately. He was in contact with various churches and charities in England, speaking from the pulpit of Spurgeon's Tabernacle in southeast London, which led to a collection worth $175. "Again things looked dark until he was invited to preach in the pulpit of Dr. Spurgeon's great church in London. A collection was taken for the minister and his boys and they were relieved from want. Rev. Jenkins spoke in churches in London, Bromley, Kent, and other places in England. He remained about six months overseas on the trip." This account is found in a tract from ca. 1936.

Charles Spurgeon had founded a large Baptist church in the London district known as The Elephant and Castle, because of a public house that stood near the junction of six major roads. Officially called the Metropolitan Tabernacle, the church was usually referred to as Spurgeon's Tabernacle. Spurgeon had died in 1892, but he was well known in the United States, where a collection of his sermons had sold hundreds of thousands of copies. Newspapers in several American cities had reprinted his sermons, and his charitable activities had attracted visits from General James Garfield, later U.S. President; the evangelist Dwight Moody; and the Fisk University Jubilee Singers who had raised funds there. The Rev. C. T. Walker of Augusta, Georgia, was known as the "black Spurgeon," but Jenkins may have known of Spurgeon from his orphanage in London's Stockwell.[3]

V. J. Charlesworth of the Stockwell orphanage wrote to the London weekly *The Baptist* on September 10, asking for contributions to help Jenkins and the boys, suggesting that "it is quite clear that he has been ill-advised in coming to this country, for he finds it impossible to appeal for help in our thoroughfares, as he hoped to have done."[4] He added that Jenkins was to visit ninety-year-old George Müller, whose orphanage had been established for many years in Bristol, and would be attending a gathering of the Young People's Society of Christian Endeavour at Stockwell.

Jenkins was to send enough money home from Britain to settle the debts.[5] He also obtained a written commendation from Sir George Williams, not a relative of Charleston's banker, but one of the founders of the Young Men's Christian Association (YMCA), who had been knighted in 1894 for his work over a period of fifty years when he had been one of the originators of the YMCA. Williams had a wide circle of friends, using the profits of his drapery business to support evangelical activities and relieve social problems in urban Britain. Williams had been Lord Shaftesbury's best friend, and his son, Howard Williams, was a member of the committee that ran London's leading orphanage, which had been founded by the Dublin-born Dr. Barnardo, who had married at Spurgeon's Tabernacle. The Bromley, Kent, mentioned by Jenkins as one of the places where he preached in 1895, was a market town on the southeastern edge of London. Sir George William's nephew (John Williams) and nephew's father-in-law (Matthew Hodder) lived there. "Matthew Hodder was very closely linked with George Williams in Y.M.C.A. matters, and the child musicians were just the sort of thing he would engage George Williams' interest in."[6] Bromley, with some twenty-five thousand inhabitants, was not yet an outer commuter suburb of London. Spurgeon had laid the foundation stone at the Bromley Baptist Church, and Matthew Hodder was the speaker at a meeting at this church on September 11, 1895, but no trace of Parson Jenkins has been found. Bromley was not unused to black visitors, for a nearby estate had been owned by Prime Minister William Pitt, and the oak tree, where he had discussed the abolition of slavery in the British Empire with William Wilberforce, was a place of pilgrimage for blacks, missionaries, and pro-black philanthropists, including the first black Bishop of west Africa, Samuel Crowther (ca. 1810–1891).[7]

Hodder, Williams, and Spurgeon had aided the black American exslave evangelist Thomas Lewis Johnson, who may have met Jenkins while working in the United States. Johnson and his brother-in-law had been trained at Spurgeon's College and both had been missionaries in the Cameroons in 1878–1879.[8] Johnson worked for the YMCA and in evangelical circles in Britain and America from 1880, speaking at Spurgeon's Tabernacle, where no trace of Jenkins has been found. The tabernacle was used for various gatherings and lectures, including at least one on phrenology, and independent sources confirm that Parson Jenkins allocated children to the different orphanage departments by the shape of their skulls.[9]

Despite the help from these British philanthropists, Charlesworth's letter annoyed at least one reader of *The Baptist*, whose response was published four weeks later on October 11, 1895. This "English Baptist" complained that Americans were rich enough and American Baptists were numerous enough to support their own appeals, and did not want any more charity "bestowed upon the impecunious representatives of wealthy America."

Parson Jenkin's adventures in England in September 1895 were reported in Charleston's *News and Courier* on September 21, in an article which repeated much of the London newspaper report, adding "Mr. Jenkins was getting successfully through his difficulties now, and that he hoped to return to Charleston about the 5th of October. His friends here will be much pleased to learn of this, as the public would much regret to see the Rev. Jenkins and his Orphanage come to grief." Sir George Williams's letter was dated September 30, 1895, indicating that Parson Jenkins was still in Britain in October 1895.

Some credence might be given to dim folk memories and to British researcher John Chilton's view that Jenkins had been in Britain between 1889 and 1891. Former orphan Paul Daniels is known to have attended a school for blacks in a small town in north Wales. He is known to have taken the middle name "Gabasie," which is said to be "Liberian" for "born on a Tuesday." He is reported to have been training for missionary work in Africa, hence the African middle name, and is also reported to have been thwarted in this scheme by the outbreak of a major war. Since all these events are well documented, it may be irresponsible to dismiss the suggestion that Daniels was sponsored in his studies in Wales by Daniel Jenkins. Jenkins had been in Wales before him, sponsored by two British missionaries living in Charleston, and an English married couple were actively helping at the Franklin Street orphanage by 1900.[10] Since Daniel Jenkins's formal education is subject to doubt, and some information had been omitted from the orphanage tracts, the recollections and speculations may well be true.

The only reference to Wales in orphanage tracts published during Parson Jenkins's lifetime is found in his own description of how the enterprise started:

> I have had to study, pray, and have the patience of a Job when tried, in order not to hurt the work of which I am head. I visited all of the leading white orphanages in Massachusetts, New York, Ohio, and other leading states of this country, also leading orphanages in London, Bristol, Liverpool, North

Wales, Scotland, then to France, and back to Canada with the eye of an eagle, watching how these orphanages were conducted.[11]

Chilton's suggestion of a short visit to north Wales between 1889 and 1891 is the most logical explanation of Parson Jenkin's British connections.[12] It also emphasizes how such influences on Edmund Jenkins, who was to spend most of his adult life in Britain, started at the earliest possible moment. It would seem reasonable to assume that Paul Daniels went to Britain with the band in 1895 and remained behind to study at the school that had influenced Jenkins.

Paul Daniels was a student at The African Training Institute, in Colwyn Bay, a small resort town on the north Wales coast, fifty-six miles from Liverpool, Britain's major port for both American and African shipping. The institute, also known as The Congo Institute, had been established in 1889 by the Rev. William Hughes, who had worked as a missionary in the Congo. The institute trained black students to be practical evangelists, studying medicine, printing, tailoring, carpentry, and other skills that would make them welcome in the mission field. Daniels was one of fewer than three dozen students at Colwyn Bay, for it was a small concern, dependent on charity from supporters, who were found mainly in Wales. Hughes was able to obtain the support of influential people, including Henry Morton Stanley, the Welsh-American explorer, and King Leopold of the Belgians, who had control of the Congo at this time. News of the institute had spread in the black world, encouraged by Hughes's visit to west Africa in 1893.[13] Local committees were formed in Sierra Leone, the Gambia, Nigeria, and the Gold Coast, and news of the institute traveled to Liberia, the Cameroons, the Congo, South Africa, and to the Zambesi, as well as to Grenada, Jamaica, and Guiana in the Caribbean.[14] Thomas Lewis Johnson had close links with it from 1892, and the American black Joseph Morford studied at the institute before taking up missionary work in Nigeria. The institute was aided by Alfred L. Jones, the shipping, finance, and tropical products entrepreneur who owned the Elder, Dempster steamship line, whose interest in the welfare of black Americans included Johnson, and visiting blacks such as the nineteen from Tennessee who were emigrating to Liberia by way of England in mid-1893.[15]

2. Daniel Joseph Jenkins, ca. 1910. *Courtesy André Woods of Charleston, S.C.*

It would appear that Parson Jenkins was back in New York in December 1895, for the tract from 1913 quotes from an article entitled "Orphans Under A Cloud," by George R. Scott, dated December 12, 1895, which was published in *The Witness*. The quotes from this undiscovered article describe Jenkins, a well-built, six-foot-seven-inch black clergyman recently returned from a period in London, in such an unlikely way that one must assume journalistic license:

> At my desk, the other day, sat a thin, kind-looking colored man. He is not old in years, but nevertheless has a care-worn look. The gentleman alluded to is a wonder in his way, a Negro preacher, who is doing his best, without any aid from the State or from the City, to feed and clothe destitute children, at Charleston, S.C. The Rev. D. J. Jenkins is the originator of the Greenwood Orphan Industrial Farm and Jenkins Orphanage Institute.

Scott's article brought in over $1,800.

Scott and his son W. G. Scott continued to support the Jenkins orphanage. The Charleston City Council started granting money to the orphanage from 1897, when it gave two hundred dollars. This support was not overly generous, but white support for the black waifs of Charleston continued, the amounts increasing at intervals, at a time when race relations in the United States soured. Politicians in the South sought support among the poor and often semiliterate whites, and campaigned on a basis of white supremacy, Negrophobia, and race chauvinism. Votes were obtained by anti-black legislation. In 1895 the "Grandfather Clause," which had originated in Louisiana, restricted the voting of illiterates by enfranchising only those illiterates whose grandfathers had been entitled to vote. Black illiterates, the descendants of voteless slaves, thus had no votes unless they paid taxes. Semiliterate blacks were rejected by white local election management who manipulated the literacy test, enfranchising semiliterate whites but not blacks. Requirements to present tax certificates were manipulated to exclude other black voters. South Carolina had a sizeable tax-paying and literate black community, so it was the first state to introduce a party convention system that excluded minorities. The black policemen, judges, administrators, and officials of Parson Jenkins's youth were replaced by whites, and black legislators became rare during Edmund Jenkins's childhood, finally disappearing from the state legislature in 1902.

The reform school section of the orphanage had begun by May 1896, when the roll listed 536 children, eight teachers, and two laborers. The industrial farm at Ladson had opened by May 7, 1898, the date of the first copy of *The Charleston Messenger* that has been traced.[16] The paper is well printed, and has national and international news content. A single copy cost five cents; an annual subscription was $1.50. The paper described itself as "The best advertising medium in the city of Charleston to reach 35,000 colored and 35,000 white people. An advertisement or a subscription to it means aid to the colored orphans of Charleston." The paper also claims that it "Bursts the news into 37 States and in England."

This was not the only link with Britain, for the paper carries an advertisement by the orphanage that states that it was the sole U.S. agent for the British band instruments of A. Collins of London. Abraham Collins's brass band instrument company was established in 1865 and was based in London's Shaftesbury Avenue from 1891, where it supplied the needs of the thousands of brass bands in Britain.[17] Collins's business merged with another company, and all records were accidentally destroyed in 1976. The destruction of many of the orphanage's files in two fires in the 1930s has made it impossible to trace the beginnings of this connection.

The paper also contains an announcement of the funeral parlor business of Harleston and Wilson of 119 Calhoun Street, a few minutes walk from Palmetto Street. This enterprise had been founded by Edwin Gilliard Harleston, a Florida black, whose daughter Eloise C. Harleston was to have close ties with the Jenkins family and the orphanage. Her sister Sylvia Harleston married a Lawrence who was the organist at Charleston's Plymouth Congregational Church[18] and their son William Lawrence, born in Charleston in 1897, was to have a respected career in music.[19]

The arson of a black schoolhouse on February 21, 1898, and the death of two pupils in the fire were commemorated by a forty-line poem by Jos. A. Smith published in this edition of Jenkins's paper:

Heavenly Father will it be long
Before these fiends stop their cursed wrong?

For they are always on our track,
ready to smite, because our skins are black.

The poem ends with the plea:

Our race shall be free from they
Who try to take our rights away.

In November 1898 several blacks were killed near Phoenix, S.C., because they were trying to vote.[20] Some railway travel was segregated by state legislation in 1898, and this legislation extended to all trains by 1900.

In the summer of 1899 Paul Daniels left Colwyn Bay's African Training Institute, unable to travel to Africa due to the buildup of military transports of British troops journeying to South Africa for the expected war with the Dutch-speaking republics. The news was published in the London monthly *The African Times* of June 5, 1899, which reported details of the annual meeting of Hughes's school, and added:

At the close of the present academical year, two of the students will return to their native homes: one to Freetown, Sierra Leone, as assistant to the Rev. M. T. G. Lawson (a coloured pastor); the other to Charleston, South Carolina, as assistant to the Rev. Mr. Jenkins (coloured superintendent of the orphanage for children in that State).

CHAPTER 3

HE COULD PLAY ANY
INSTRUMENT IN THE
BAND

By 1900 Parson Jenkins was the minister of the Bethlehem Baptist Church near Kingstree, S.C., of another church at Williamsburg, as well as of the Palmetto Street church in Charleston.[1] The orphanage was accepting "half orphans," children with only one parent, such as Amos Mordecai White, who recalled that his mother enrolled him since she believed that the orphanage offered better opportunities than she could.[2] He also recalled that the orphanage in 1900 had black and white teachers. "Most of the teachers at the school were Negro. Three were white, two from England (Mr. and Mrs. Mann) and one from Charleston (Mr. Dorsey) who taught piano and organ music. He also taught Mr. Jenkins' children who became very fine musicians."[3]

Stirling Herbert Jenkins played the trumpet with the orphanage brass band, and later at the University of Pennsylvania where he studied dentistry.[4] Nathaniel and Joseph Jenkins both played the trombone. The instruction at Franklin Street at first was under the direction of an outsider, but, as John Dowling, a lifelong associate of Jenkins and the Orphanage, remembered, "After he got his band started, why he didn't have to hire any more band leaders because they grew up and as a boy advanced enough to take charge, why he would take charge of the band. After the first ten years we didn't have to hire any more musical directors."[5]

The musical director at the beginning was P. M. "Hattsie" Logan, whose sister Anna and brother Jimmy were musicians in Charleston.[6] Another teacher was Francis Eugene Mikell, who may have studied at Avery Institute in Charleston, the city's leading school for blacks.[7] Parson Jenkins's children went to Avery, which had been established in 1866 by the American Missionary Association and one of the Free Persons of Color, Francis Cardozo, who had been South Carolina's Secretary of State after the Civil War and had British connections through his studies at Glasgow University.[8]

Two of the musical directors who had first played with the band were William Leroy Blake and Alonzo Hardy. Blake specialized on brass instruments and was an expert on the tuba. He had an excellent singing voice. Hardy was also a brass specialist, notably with the trumpet. The emphasis on brass band instruments at Franklin Street was not unusual at this time, for brass bands were not uncommon in America, where ten thousand municipalities had supported their own civic bands in 1890.[9]

The other vocational aspects of the orphanage continued, with shoe repairing, laundry, job printing, and bread baking activities at Franklin Street. The return of Paul Daniels released Parson Jenkins from some of the daily routine, and, from 1902 he was assisted with the secretarial work by Eloise Harleston. The farm at Ladson was used for delinquent children "Criminals and little vicious boys . . . made to earn their own bread by the sweat of their brow," as Jenkins described them in the 1898 *Charleston Messenger*. The reform school at Franklin Street was for "little orphan and destitute boys, who are convicted in the Police Court for trivial offences."[10] Without the Jenkins Orphanage the fate of these children would be far worse, for the same tract warns, "Save your children and those under your care from the jail and state penitentiary. Parents and guardians must act or to the chain-gang their boys will go."

Parson Jenkins did not encourage his own children to mix with the inmates, but such connections were made in the brass band. In 1904 the band, with Nathaniel Jenkins, Alonzo Hardy, and sixteen others, led by Logan, went to England.[11] In 1906 Parson Jenkins, Eloise Harleston, and another black woman went to England.[12] It is possible that the band went with them, but it is known that in the industrial mill town of Wigan, Lancashire, in November 1906 Miss Harleston gave birth to a girl child. Baby Olive was left in the care of the English midwife who registered the birth, giving no father's name. The father was Parson Daniel Jenkins.[13] His connection with

Wigan is unknown, other than it was one of the few English towns that supported William Hughes's Institute in Colwyn Bay.[14]

The orphanage's brass band was not the sole musical influence on Edmund Jenkins, for the "teachers in the employ of the Society write personal letters to their friends, and they also give parlor entertainments and concerts, by which they raise quite a sum."[15] Black workers associations in Charleston, with their bands, took part in the Labor Day parade in the city, an event that Edmund Jenkins was later to describe as the highlight of the year for Charleston blacks.[16] The 1913 tract includes a photograph of a group of twenty-eight musicians with the bass drum painted "Jenkins Orphan Brass Band And Orchestra, Charleston, SC," and this group includes violins and a string bass. It is uncertain who taught the violin to Edmund Jenkins, who performed on it at concerts at Franklin Street. The teenage Edmund Jenkins was also skilled on the clarinet and the piano. His tutor on the clarinet is unknown; the piano lessons were probably from Dorsey, or from Will Lawrence's teacher, J. Donovan Moore.

There were vocal groups at the orphanage, from quartets to choirs, and Edmund had training in vocal techniques. "At 14 he could play capably any instrument used in the band."[17] His studies at Avery Institute with the children of Charleston's black elite included French, Latin, science, and music, but the institute's records have been destroyed.[18]

The deterioration in the daily life of black Americans, disfranchised, subject to violence, lynching, and outrage, all encouraged by the indifference of white authority, had reached a new level with the September 1906 race riots in Atlanta, Georgia, when black lives and property were destroyed. In August 1908 Springfield, Illinois, was the site of further race riots. Edward Jenkins, Edmund's brother, died in 1908. His vegetable dealing business was possibly continued by his widow, Julia.[19]

In 1908 Edmund Jenkins left his parents' home to continue his studies in Atlanta, Georgia.[20] Edmund attended Morehouse College, where he studied under Benjamin Brawley, whose father E. M. Brawley was one of the Free Persons of Color and had been responsible for the organization of the black Baptist church in the Carolinas after the Civil War. Benjamin Brawley had attended Morehouse College, then named the Atlanta Baptist College, in

1895, and had been graduated from it in 1901 when he was nineteen. He taught English and Latin there from 1902, and was professor of English in 1906. From 1910 to 1912 he was in Washington, D.C., as professor of English at Howard University, and returned to Morehouse College in 1912 to take up the position of dean.[21] In 1926 Brawley recalled his first meeting with Edmund Jenkins:

> I well remember him as he came into the room now more than sixteen years ago. I can see again the tight little black coat with the dozen medals that even then he had won, all in full array. Evidently here was something different from the ordinary boy who came to enter the academy, and for the moment I could hardly repress a smile. For him, however, it was serious business; so I examined him and assigned him to a class. He remained at Morehouse six years. For two of those years I was away. One day, however, on passing down a street in Boston, I saw him leading the little boys of the Jenkins Orphan Band. He often had to direct them and sometimes he told me that the work was very taxing; yet I could not forget how much it did to give him the all-round equipment that he afterwards possessed. On my return to Atlanta I found that, under the tutelage of Mr. Harreld, he had become even more proficient. With three instruments—the piano, the violin, and the clarinet—his acquaintance was not less than masterly. Even so we did not appreciate him sufficiently. But when is genius fully appreciated?[22]

Edmund Jenkins's music teacher was Kemper Harreld, who was born in 1885 and had studied music in Berlin, Germany.[23] He was a violinist, and was head of Morehouse's Department of Music, but also taught in other black institutions in Atlanta. Possibly his most famous pupil was Fletcher Henderson, a graduate chemist whose orchestra was to contain many notable black jazz musicians during the 1920s and 1930s, and who was to be the arranger of the music for the Benny Goodman orchestra.[24] Harreld directed the orchestra at Morehouse[25] and, like Brawley, kept in contact with Edmund Jenkins years after he had completed his studies in Atlanta. "Mr. Harreld took an active personal interest in Edmund's musical development, and the youngster became an important factor in the music life of the college, which included a splendid symphony orchestra and glee club."[26]

A friend of the Jenkins family, Mr. T. L. Grant of Brooklyn, New York, recalled an incident that shows some of Edmund's musical activities during the vacations from Morehouse:

> In the summer of 1912 while spending some time in Atlantic City, one day I saw a man and a small boy walking by my hotel in the uniform of the Jenkins Orphanage Band. Of course I became interested and when they came closer, I discovered Rev. Paul Daniels and Edmund T. Jenkins. Edmund was an ill boy, I found out, but after I took them into the hotel and have the doctor give him a physic, he was relieved; and that night at a concert the Band gave, Edmund played his instrument better than ever.[27]

Willie "The Lion" Smith, pianist, composer, and raconteur, recalled the Jenkins Orphanage Band in New York about this time:

> They had a kind of circus band that marched up and down the streets of Harlem. They'd play concerts on street corners and then pass the hat. They sometimes had as many as twenty pieces and none of the kids were over fifteen years of age.[28]

The band took summer tours north, and went to Florida most winters, to collect donations from the tourists. In Jacksonville they were able to stay with Parson Jenkins's sister Dora who arranged the permits from police, chamber of commerce, and town hall, authorizing the band to play on the street. In other cities the band called on friends of the orphanage, subscribers to *The Charleston Messenger*, church associates of Parson Jenkins, and other black sympathizers. Parson Jenkins was known as The Orphanage Man, and his band, including Edmund, played at national events such as the 1909 inaugural parade of President Taft, according to the 1913 tract, which also says that one-quarter of the institution's income was from the band "giving concerts and accepting jobs for playing at great gatherings, especially during the summer months, in the North. Invitations from all portions of the country are received, and, whenever the expenses are guaranteed, with a little surplus for the Orphanage, they go."

In September 1912 Edmund's mother died.[29] Only four of the eleven children were alive at this time.[30] Stirling Jenkins, who had a dental practice in Washington, D.C., had died in 1912, and only Edmund, Lena, Roxie, and Mildred survived their mother. Roxie ran away from Charleston in 1913, marrying Amos White, who had studied printing at Franklin Street and also played the cornet, leading one of the brass bands which, he was later to recall, played "cakewalks."[31] Lena had married Percy Howard, and had one child, Livingston.

After the death of his first wife, Parson Jenkins married Eloise Harleston, first living at 18 Franklin Street and later moving to a larger house at 34 Magazine Street, on the northern side of the jail. This house was given to the Jenkins's by Miss Harleston's undertaker father.[32] By 1913 the orphanage had telephone number 77 and was taking large advertising space in the city directories. It published an illustrated tract, which has been dated to 1913 as it contains details of the city's contributions—now reaching one thousand dollars a year—up to and including 1912.

Before detailing another aspect of Edmund Jenkins's musical education during his years in Atlanta, it may be wise to look at the music scene in the United States before and during Edmund's youth.

CHAPTER **4**

THE METROPOLITAN OPERA AND PREJUDICE EDUCATE HIM

The first purely American form of stage entertainment was the minstrel show, which developed in the theaters and music halls of the northeastern states. Thomas D. Rice, a white entertainer, introduced his "Jim Crow" dance to New York in 1832 and to London in 1836. White men in black face captured the nation's imagination. By the 1840s the minstrel show had become formalized, and troupes appeared at the same venue for years. Edwin Christy's minstrels were very popular, singing the songs of Stephen Foster to thousands in America and Europe. Over one million copies of the sheet music of Foster's *Old Folks At Home* were sold.[1]

The music of America's four million slaves was not noted in any truly musicological manner until the Civil War, when northern whites, working among the black communities on the sea islands off the Georgia and South Carolina coast, noted and published "plantation songs."[2] Another change in American music came in 1865 when New York-born Tony Pastor with exminstrel manager Sam Sharpley welcomed women customers to their New Jersey variety theater. From 1881 Pastor introduced one or two new songs nearly every week. Pastor used the French word *vaudeville* to describe his shows, and this concept was further developed by the partnership of Keith and Proctor who appealed to a middle-class audience with nonstop entertainment and a chain of theaters in different locations.[3] The shows included anything that might tempt the passer-by into the theater, and the acts needed cheap music.[4]

Irish people were the source of humor in Ferguson and Mack's San Francisco presentations in 1882, and later New Yorkers were amused by Harrigan and Hart. Harrigan's shows were often pivoted on a clash between blacks and Irish in New York. Toward the end of the century the public showed less interest in Harrigan's style of entertainment, and his last production was in 1903, by which time black composers such as Gussie Lord Davis and Will Marion Cook, and black entertainers such as Bert Williams, had become established in the music business in America, although they had to conform to the image of blacks created by the whites in minstrelsy.[5]

The tin-foil phonograph developed by Edison in the late 1870s made little impact on the American public for ten years, when it was exploited commercially as a coin-operated entertainment. The quality of the recordings and of the reproduction of those recordings was poor. Phonograph cylinders were restricted to brass bands, cornet soli, and whatever else its limited equipment could record.[6] In 1893 Emile Berliner established the disc-playing gramophone, and by 1898 had contracted Edison's most popular artist, John Philip Sousa's U.S. Marine Band, whose brass band recordings were available in many American towns. Playing equipment was available on the installment plan by mail order.

Gianni Bettini in New York showed that the recording industry was capable of recording serious music and sold recordings of Metropolitan Opera stars at four to twelve times the price of other records. By the beginning of the twentieth century recording and pressing plants were established in Europe, and in March 1902 the first truly musical sounds available from the gramophone were recorded in Milan, Italy, by Enrico Caruso.[7] In England, in April 1909 the first large-scale orchestral recordings were made; the American recording industry continued to produce little material other than the tried-and-tested arias, brass bands, instrumental soli, and comic-talk records.[8]

Serious music had to be heard in public concerts, and less serious music was also available in public, with bands playing in parks, at seaside and other resorts, and in the streets. The growing industrial technology of America with the inventiveness of mainly German craftsmen produced mechanical musical instruments, but of a size and price that they were found mainly in bars and other places of entertainment. Amateur music making between friends, encouraged by the parlor piano and other domestic instruments available on easy credit terms to black and white Americans, was a regular feature of "decent" homes.[9] If the music lover was unable to play an instrument it was possible to pedal a Pianola, choosing paper piano rolls of classical and popular melodies.

Vaudeville in America and music hall in Britain featured varied programs, which in Britain emphasized regional humor and dialect. The melting pot of the American cities, which had separate ethnic theaters, enabled successful and popular entertainers to travel to other towns with their acts, which not only spread a popular song quickly but also supported the chains of theaters. There were links between American and British theaters, because the shared language made contact easier between owners, agents, and performers—and, they hoped, between artist and audience. The urban population needed cheap entertainment, which from 1892 was catered for by songs such as Charles K. Harris's *After the Ball* the "first million seller to be conceived as a million seller, and marketed as a million seller."[10] The 1890s were years of change in the United States, as it grew to be the world's leading industrial nation by 1900.

The development of black music in the 1890s is to be seen in what is usually regarded as the first authentic black contribution to American popular music, namely "ragtime" or "cakewalk." Ragtime did not get into print until 1897.[11] Toward the end of that year white Ben Harney, who had accompanied black entertainers Tom Mack and Strap Hill, published his *Ragtime Instructor* manual, introducing ragtime to polite society. This black music became respectable, and whites played, published, enjoyed, and exploited it. A number of tours of Europe by Sousa, especially his rendition of Frederick "Kerry" Mills's *At a Georgia Camp Meeting* of 1897, spread cakewalk syncopation outside the United States. Sousa's own compositions, also well known across America and Europe, were arranged by his trombonist Arthur Pryor, who left Sousa in 1900 to run his own band.

Gussie Davis, a Cincinnati black who died in 1899, wrote sentimental ballads. His great hit *In the Baggage Coach Ahead* sold over one million copies.[12] Will Marion Cook, "an erratic genius, a man of more than ordinary talent"[13] seems to have been unable to obtain lasting popularity, perhaps because "he protested against the minstrel tradition on the one hand and the imitation of florid classics on the other."[14] Cook was to be involved with Edmund Jenkins. The son of two graduates of Oberlin University, where he was to study as a youth, Cook went to Germany to complete his violin studies. He returned from Berlin in the 1890s and studied with Dvořák in New York. In 1898 he wrote the music for *Clorindy: The Origin of the Cake-Walk*, to words by the black poet Paul Dunbar.

The minstrel show traditions continued, especially in rural America, but the first black show written and produced by blacks was the 1898 *A Trip to Coontown* by Bob Cole and Billy Johnson. Cook and Dunbar's *Clorindy* followed this, and, in 1902 Cook wrote *In Dahomey* which featured the dancing of Bert Williams. The show traveled to London in 1903, where it played for seven months, attracting the attention of George Bernard Shaw, who suggested that Williams should play Ftatateeta, the nurse in *Caesar and Cleopatra*.[15]

The center for music and entertainment in America was New York, and the black entertainers gathered at the Marshall Hotel between 6th and 7th Avenues on West 53rd Street, for Harlem was not then a black area. Cook, Dunbar (whose biography was written by Benjamin Brawley), Cole, James Weldon Johnson, and his brother Rosamond were the leaders of this group.[16] Bob Cole's 1902 *Under the Bamboo Tree* sold thousands of copies, and Cole and the two Johnsons went to Europe. The Johnsons were from Jacksonville, Florida, and were probably known to Parson Jenkins. The Johnsons and Cole journeyed through France and Belgium, and in Brussels they met a South Carolina black named Woodson who had been in Europe for eighteen years, seven of them as stage manager at the Palais d'Eté.[17] In London they appeared at the Palace Theater. Johnson later wrote that "It is a wise general rule for American Negroes in Europe to steer clear of their white fellow-countrymen. . . . "[18]

Working overseas provided opportunities for entertainers; black American entertainers were encouraged by the lack of U.S.-style restrictions and the more amenable white theater owners they found outside the United States. West Indians such as Bert Williams saw opportunities in the United States, but facilities in the Caribbean were limited. Black acts had traveled to Britain from the 1830s, when Philadelphia black Frank Johnson had taken his orchestra to London in 1837.[19] The Fisk University Jubilee Singers had been in England in 1873 and in 1875. James Bland, who wrote *Carry Me Back to Old Virginny* in 1875, went to England in 1880 with a black minstrel group, and remained in Europe until 1890.[20] Black shows traveled widely; Orpheus McAdoo was in South Africa in 1889 and owned a theater in Australia by the end of the century.[21] Frederick J. Loudin, from Ohio, had joined the Fisk singers for their 1875 trip to England, and later ran the group as a separate commercial enterprise on a world tour. Loudin was resident in London by 1900.

In 1905, at one of Proctor's New York City theaters, the black theatrical promoter Joe Jordan featured a group entitled The Memphis Students under the direction of Will Marion Cook. "This organization was the first truly genuine Negro playing unit; like the original Jubilee Singers, it blazed a trail to Europe its first season and was overwhelmingly successful in its demonstration of 'the new music.' "[22]

In December 1907 *die Schwarze Nachtigall* ("The Black Nightingale") Arabella Fields recorded in Germany for Anker Records.[23] In 1910 Jordan was in Germany and toured British music halls, returning to Chicago by 1911. His group, King and Bailey's Chocolate Drops, or part of them, may have played at the Brussels world fair of 1910.[24]

The ragtime boom was nearly over when Irving Berlin's 1911 composition *Alexander's Ragtime Band* sold hundreds of thousands of copies in its first year. This song revived the name ragtime, but not the rhythm, for Berlin's hit is merely slightly syncopated. By 1911 the ragtime period, which had created some fine melodies and excellent rhythms, was over, for the harmonic structure of ragtime was limited. The future of much American music was to be affected by the experiments of the schooled brass player W. C. Handy, who started investigating the blues form in 1909 in Mississippi. His amalgamation of folk blues themes and band orchestrations in 1909 helped elect E. H. Crump to be mayor of Memphis, but his *Mr. Crump*, retitled *The Memphis Blues*, was not published until 1912.

Seriously minded black musicians had been encouraged by wealthy white New Yorker Mrs. Jeanette M. Thurber who, in 1885, founded the racially mixed National Conservatory of Music. Mrs. Thurber had been instrumental in obtaining the services of Antonín

Dvořák as director of the conservatory from September 1892. Black tenor Harry T. Burleigh is credited with introducing black songs to Dvořák, whose Czech origins in the vast and polyglot Austro-Hungarian Empire made him aware of the musical culture of minorities. In May 1894 Dvořák drew attention to the treasury of black music available to composers in America, and this observation, printed in a New York newspaper just after Edmund Jenkins's birth, was to be a great influence on him in adult life. Dvořák's *From the New World* symphony composed in 1893 is supposed to contain American Indian and black themes, but Dvořák regarded it, and all other music he composed in America and Britain, as genuine music from Bohemia.[25] He was not as interested in black themes as Burleigh, Cook, and other black music students might have expected, for he refused an offer to spend the summer of 1893 in South Carolina, preferring to pass the vacation in a Czech settlement in Iowa.[26]

The spirit of nationalism grew in the 1890s, as empires expanded and many peoples in Europe and America felt that they were superior to other groups and nations. This nationalism spread to the music world and influenced most of Edmund Jenkins's tutors. Ancient folk music and traditional themes were traced, noted, and orchestrated, giving ammunition to George Bernard Shaw, then a music critic for the London press, who suggested that "the poorer composers, unable to invent interesting themes for their works in sonata form, gladly availed themselves of the licence to steal popular airs."[27] Americans, aware that they were a mixture of nationalities, considered how they were to produce American music. Mrs. Thurber was anxious to have Dvořák produce an American composition and suggested that he use Longfellow's poem *Hiawatha*, which he had read in a Czech translation. She wanted a libretto for an opera from this American Indian theme, to which Dvořák would add the music, making an "American" composition. They failed to anticipate Samuel Coleridge-Taylor, a black Englishman, who made a cantata of Longfellow's poem.

Coleridge-Taylor was to be a major influence on Edmund Jenkins and on other black Americans. His father was a west African who had studied in England and was a medical student in London. He returned to Africa soon after Samuel's birth in London in 1875, and his English wife moved to Croydon, ten miles south of central London, where the child's musical studies were encouraged, leading to further study under Charles Villiers Stanford at London's Royal College of Music. Samuel Coleridge-Taylor was introduced to black music by Paul Dunbar, who was in London in 1896,[28] and by Loudin's Jubilee Singers.[29] Loudin was the London link between Mrs. Mamie Hilyer of Washington, D.C., and Coleridge-Taylor. Mrs. Hilyer and other black Americans formed a Coleridge-Taylor Choral Society in 1901, for the young black composer had not been prevented from artistic success by the color prejudice that so restricted the American blacks, and he was idolized in the United States. In 1903 the society performed his *Hiawatha* in Washington, and in 1904 he crossed the Atlantic to visit his admirers, who knew of his acceptance in Britain and of the help given him by Edward Elgar, the leading composer of the English nationalist school.

One of the contacts he made during this 1904 visit was with Clarence Cameron White, a black composer and violinist who had attended Oberlin. White traveled to London to study with Coleridge-Taylor, who was teaching at a small music school in south London's Crystal Palace. Another American contact led to a commission for *Twenty-Four Negro Melodies Transcribed for Piano*, and Coleridge-Taylor acknowledged his debt to the recently deceased Loudin in his foreword. The U.S. edition of this work had a biographical note by Booker T. Washington.

In 1906 Coleridge-Taylor again crossed the Atlantic and met the accompanist of the Coleridge-Taylor Choral Society, Miss Mary Europe. Her brother James Reese Europe was a successful music promoter, responsible for many opportunities for black musicians in America, organizing bands and orchestras for black and white patrons in New York and elsewhere in the North. He established the "Clef Club," which produced a black music concert at Carnegie Hall in May 1912, and also directed "Europe's Society Orchestra." This orchestra was to help develop the latest craze in America— public dancing. This spread in the 1910s, giving work to thousands of black and white musicians. Europe's orchestra was employed by Vernon and Irene Castle, and Europe and the Castles invented the most popular dance craze, the fox trot. Sheet music showed Europe's black face; the recordings issued by Victor showed both Europe's and the Castle's names, including a February 1914 disc entitled *Castle Walk*,[30] which was written by Europe and Ford Dabney. Dabney was yet another American black musician who had worked abroad, having been official court musician in Haiti from 1904 until 1907.[31]

As Edmund Jenkins was growing up in Charleston, and during his studies at Avery and later in Atlanta, the major influences on blacks interested in serious music were Coleridge-Taylor, Dvořák, Will Marion Cook, Cole, the Johnsons, Joe Jordan, and Jim Europe. Following the expiration of old patents, and encouraged by the requirements of dance music, there had been vast improvements in the disc-playing gramophones from 1910 to 1920, which increased sales. In 1902 Victor had recorded *The Dinwiddie Colored Quartet* and issued the results on single-sided discs, but few black recordings were made until 1920. Edmund Jenkins would have had access to the recordings of the New York Metropolitan Opera, which were released by Victor on their Red Seal label. The Metropolitan Opera—and race prejudice—supplied the next aspect of Jenkins's education in Atlanta.

Morehouse College was one of five black colleges established in Atlanta by 1886. The city was an intellectual center for black Americans, which, by the time Jenkins was studying with Brawley and Harreld, was of particular musical importance. A black Congregational minister, the Rev. Henry Hugh Proctor, was head of the First Congregational Church on Houston Street, Atlanta, and "his church choir was regarded as 'one of the best in all the city'; it had not only a professional director, Professor P. M. Thompson, but also a professional organist, Miss Nellie Askew, and a cornetist, E. T. Jenkins."[32] Edmund Jenkins's name appears in a list of the church officials in the program of a concert given by the Tuskegee Band Orchestra and Glee Club in Atlanta on Friday, March 22, 1912.[33] The concert was part of the Atlanta Colored Music Festival Association, established by Proctor in July 1910 to bring to the city "the best musical talent of the race," after he became aware that women in his congregation were prepared to pose as servants in order to attend the week of performances of the New York Metropolitan Opera, which was an annual event in Atlanta.

How many concerts and festival events were to involve Edmund Jenkins as performer or member of the audience must remain speculation, for his work with the orphanage band took him away from the city during vacations. The concert of February 10, 1911, and that of March 22, 1912, when his name appears in the program, should not have been affected by band travels. The program indicates something of the black community of Atlanta during Jenkins's six years in the city. Proctor's church had helped "in the readjustment of the relations between the races after the riot of 1906."[34] The program says that the church believed "in missionary work, not only in Africa, but also in Atlanta, and sends out workers in back alleys, hospitals and prisons," and had a library of three thousand volumes—the only public library for Atlanta's fifty-two thousand black citizens.

Harry Burleigh and Anita Patti Brown, later friends of Edmund Jenkins, were performing at Proctor's third festival in August 1912. The music played included works by Burleigh, Cook, and Coleridge-Taylor. The 1913 concert was held on July 3 and 4, to commemorate the fiftieth anniversary of the abolition of slavery in the United States. Roland Hayes, Anita Patti Brown, Clarence Cameron White, and the Fisk Jubilee Singers performed. Coleridge-Taylor, who had died in England in September 1912, had his masterpiece *Hiawatha* featured at the grand concert on July 4.[35]

Edmund Jenkins left Morehouse College in May 1914. As Brawley recollected twelve years later, "He told me that his father was going to take the band to London and that he would have to leave immediately. I shall not soon forget the next two afternoons. He had always loved tennis, and he played as if he would never play again. Then he went."[36]

Edmund Jenkins was not to return to the United States for over six years.

CHAPTER 5

"MY BOY WILL HAVE TO LEAVE VERY SOON"

Edmund Jenkins was called from his studies at Morehouse to take part in the Anglo-American Exposition, one of the large and fashionable exhibitions organized by the experienced Hungarian Imre Kiralfy and his three sons at an exhibition site four miles from the center of London. The exhibition site was in west London's Shepherd's Bush district. It had been built for the Franco-British Exhibition of 1908 and extended the same year to include a stadium for 150,000 spectators to watch the Olympic Games. The 1908 events had attracted well over eight million people and the 1914 exhibition was scheduled to entertain millions, too.[1]

Kiralfy's theme was "to celebrate the centenary of peace and progress in the arts, sciences, and industries of the United States of America and the British Empire." Imre Kiralfy was in the United States in February 1914, arranging exhibits, side shows and other matters. Through the Dayton, Ohio, offices of the theatrical impressarios Jules and Max Hurtig, who operated the Colonial Theater in that city, Parson Jenkins was in regular contact with the exhibition plans. Kiralfy must have seen obvious popular appeal in the Jenkins "piccaninny" band and may have known of their vaudeville act from their London appearance in 1904. The band's appeal was that the members were small and black, for Jules Hurtig's letter to Jenkins on April 16, 1914 states, "This time I feel quite sure that we can go through with it but in some what more in a dignified manner and if we can make satisfactory arrangements and

the terms reasonable the Band will be used only for Concert pur-
poses for the Exposition patrons." Hurtig had already contacted
Parson Jenkins from New York in February, and other surviving
telegrams indicate that the band was to have a ten-week engagement starting on May 14, 1914, with all transportation and board
paid.[2] None of Parson Jenkins's replies has been found, but there
were difficulties arranging the transport of the band from Charleston. Originally scheduled to travel via the Clyde Line, which ran
regular sailings from Jacksonville via Charleston to New York,
there was a last-minute hitch, and in less than twenty-four hours
Jules Hurtig cabled Parson Jenkins three times, finally offering on
May 2, to pay railroad fares for the group.

There were eighteen members in the Jenkins Orphan Band in London in the summer of 1914. Billed in the exposition program as the
"American Piccaninny Band," the group included some young
men, despite Hurtig's second cable of May 1 which asked Jenkins to
"bring with you the best musicians you have of the small boys." Six
picture postcards of the band, described as the "Famous Piccaninny
Band," were on sale at the exposition. The leader was Logan,
named "Professor" by the boys, usually shortened to "Fess."
Edmund Jenkins played the clarinet; Emerson Harper played the
other clarinet; William Benford, although not ten-years-old, played
the tuba. As orphanage records indicate that Benford entered the
institution in late May 1913, his presence in London one year later
indicates the intensity of the instruction at Franklin Street and the
magnitude of his talent. Another youngster in the band was the
"director," Johnny Garlington, who conducted the band and whose
features, dwarfed by a large uniform cap, appeared on one of the
souvenir postcards. Jacob Frazier may have been one of the two
trombonists; the two trombone players may instead have been the
brothers Ed and Jacob Patrick. The cornet players may have
included Alonzo Mills, Frank Wallace, Alonzo Hardy, or Daniel
Green, but all four taught at the orphanage, and their names may
have been confused with others.

The success of the Jenkins band is indicated by the postcards on
sale at the exposition as well as by a letter of July 15, 1914, from
Leolyn Hart, the general director of the Bristol International Exhibition. He asked Parson Jenkins "Could you arrange for your 'Picka-
ninny Band' to play at this Exhibition for one week." Jenkins was

unable to accept, for the contract at the exposition was extended from the original ten weeks. Documents in Charleston indicate that Parson Jenkins did travel to Bristol, where he renewed his 1895 contacts with Müller's Homes, and that he visited Dr. Barnardo's Homes in east London, and the seamen's institute in Liverpool. He also visited Wigan with Mrs. Eloise Jenkins, visiting Nurse Layland and their daughter, Olive.[3] The affairs of the orphanage, the newspaper, and the church could not be left without his guidance for many months, and Jenkins made arrangements to leave England on the Cunard liner *Laconia*, sailing August 8, 1914.

Edmund Jenkins had been helping Logan with the direction of the band, and, apparently because he had been accepted as a student at London's Royal Academy of Music for the academic year beginning September 21, 1914, his father had to arrange a responsible replacement. Parson Jenkins wrote to the thirty-four-year-old Charleston-born Francis Eugene Mikell on July 25, 1914:

> I would like to have you here to lead the Band, as my boy will have to leave very soon. We are doing well here. This is a great country. I am compelled to go home and would like to have just such a man as you with whom to leave my Band. They play only five hours daily as you will see from the enclosed program; no work on Sunday; everybody goes to church. This would be the trip of your life if you would come to London. You would be paid in a hundred and one ways I need not mention. We are offered jobs from everywhere over here. If we had ten bands we could get work to do. If you would like to lead my Band until within one week of Christmas at which time we will be in Charleston, cable me on receipt of this letter as follows: "Jenkins, Piccaninny Band, White City, Shepherd's Bush, London, England. Can come, Mikell." On receipt of my reply, "Come at once," buy your ticket to New York via Clyde Line and I will meet you there Aug. 16th. I shall be stopping at 147 W 132nd St., and I shall send you direct to the Band.

Mikell was living at 1228 W. Duval Street in Jacksonville, Florida. Jenkins confirmed the salary at $35 per month, and listed the band's tour after their return to New York in October, through Philadel-

phia, Wilmington, Baltimore, Washington, Charlotteville, Richmond, Lynchburg, Asheville, Spartanburg, Greenville, Anderson-
ville, and Columbia. Jenkins told Mikell "This is one of the greatest
opportunities I have ever been able to offer you."

Jenkins also wrote to a former orphanage musician Brooks
Brockman in Columbia, saying that "The boys are making good.
There is a fine opportunity for you to display your great talent as a
cornetist before thousands and thousands of Europeans. I would
like to have you come at once."[4] Other letters written that weekend
included one to H. Croaxford to request tickets for P. G. Daniels
and B. Callaham from London to Charleston "on any boat you
desire sailing to New York at once,"[5] and to arrange tickets from
New York to Charleston for Mrs. Jenkins "her friend, my daughter,
and myself." The friend and Mildred Jenkins were to have their
fares paid by Parson Jenkins, suggesting that Callaham was a member of the band, being replaced by Brockman.

On July 23, 1914, typing his letter on orphanage stationery,
deleting Charleston, S.C., and typing London, England, Parson
Jenkins had written a long and serious plea to the governor of
South Carolina, Coleman Blease. Jenkins sent a copy of the two
and a half page letter to Lathan, the editor of the influential News
and Courier in Charleston.[6] Jenkins told the governor that "the sal-
vation of the South between the white and the black man lies in the
careful training of the little negro boys and girls to become honest,
upright and industrious citizens." Jenkins suggested the schools and
reformatories were better places for the young than the penitentiary, and that "Teaching the Negro to read, to write and to work,
is not going to do the white man any harm." Jenkins told Blease
that "Nine of the Councilmen of London called on me yesterday
and congratulated me on the work I am doing for my race." Since
the black waifs and strays of the Jenkins Orphanage had been
taught and trained sufficiently well "as to gain the respect of the
people of England, how much more can be done if the Governor
and Lawmakers of South Carolina would simply co-operate with
me."

The fifty-two-year-old black clergyman was using his contacts in
Britain in 1914 in as positive a manner as he had done in 1895.
However, the assassination of Archduke Franz Ferdinand in the
Balkan town of Sarajevo on June 28 had developed into an interna-
tional crisis that led, on July 28, to the declaration of war between

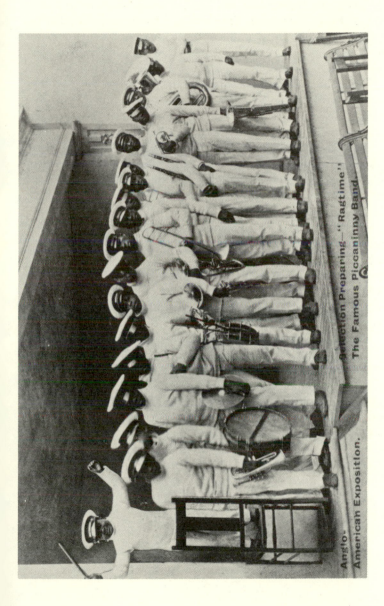

3. Jenkins Orphanage Band at the Anglo-American Exposition, London, ca. June 1914. *Original postcard in the possession of the author.*

the Austro-Hungarian Empire and Serbia, whose government was blamed for the assassination. The threat of a European war led to military preparations by Britain, and the proposed visit of King George V and his queen to the Anglo-American Exposition was canceled. Thousands took advantage of one of the sunniest summers for years as temperatures stayed in the 90°'s, and enjoyed the public holiday of Monday, August 3, 1914, at the White City Exposition and other resorts. News of the mobilization of the Imperial Russian forces came on Friday, and on Saturday, August 1, the Belgian and Netherlands forces were mobilized. On August 2 Germany declared war on Russia and marched across the frontier into Luxembourg. On the public holiday Germany declared war on France, and German armies invaded Belgium. On Tuesday, August 4, 1914, Britain declared war on Germany, whose actions had violated Belgian neutrality which Britain was bound to defend under the terms of a treaty signed a few years after Belgium's independence in 1830.

As the war scare built up Jenkins was able to return the favor of 1895 when Augustine Smythe had helped the band out of trouble at Bow Street. "The war broke out and Jenkins was able to assist several prominent Charlestonians stranded by the money confusion. They were unable to cash checks but he was paid in gold and loaned money to get them out of the country."[7] Two thousand Americans were in financial trouble in London alone that last week of July 1914,[8] including, it has been suggested, the girls of the elite white private school Ashley Hall, which was minutes away from Palmetto Street. Mrs. McBee, the headmistress, supported Parson Jenkins's orphanage for most of her life.

The Anglo-American Exposition closed quietly on August 11, 1914. The band returned to the United States by October 31, 1914, the date of the second copy of *The Charleston Messenger* that has been located,[9] for there is no mention of the months in London or of the plans that had to be aborted due to the beginning of World War I.

CHAPTER 6

AN ENGAGING
KNOWLEDGE OF
ORCHESTRAL EFFECT

The Royal Academy of Music, where Edmund Jenkins registered for the academic year beginning on September 21, 1914, was the first professional school of music in England. Founded in 1822, the Royal Academy of Music was based on the concept of a music school first noted by Charles Burney in 1774, following his visit to Italy where he had seen orphan schools produce first-rate musicians. The Royal Academy had grown out of cramped quarters and had moved to a site at York Gate in the Marylebone Road, backing on to Regent's Park, and near Madame Tussaud's waxworks and the railway station at Baker Street. This site had been occupied before 1911 by an orphanage.

There were, and had been, several other music schools in London, such as the Crystal Palace School of Art, where Coleridge-Taylor had been teaching in 1905, and his old school, the Royal College of Music, which was presided over by his old tutor, Sir Charles Villiers Stanford. Continental Europe was richer in music schools than England, and England was poorer in musical achievement, than Italy, Germany, or France in the nineteenth century. The end of the century had, however, seen the beginning of international fame for Edward Elgar, who had attended no academic music school. Germany, which had provided the musical training for Cook and Harreld, also provided the schooling for many musicians in Britain at this time, including those who were to influence Edmund Jenkins. Stanford at the Royal College, and Alexander

Mackenzie, the principal of the Royal Academy of Music, had both studied in Germany, which was "the pattern for those few English composers who overcame the prevailing apathy and amateurism of English musical life in the latter half of Victoria's reign, to become tolerably decent professionals."[1]

Mackenzie had been the principal at the Royal Academy of Music for twenty-six years when Edmund Jenkins paid his fourteen guineas (£14.70, or $75) fee on September 14, 1914. Jenkins's main study was to be composition, under the direction of Frederick Corder. Corder had studied at the academy and then traveled to Cologne where he received training under Hiller until 1878, acquiring a lifelong love of Wagner. Corder's translations of three of Wagner's operas were the first published in England. Corder became a professor at the academy in 1886, and he and Mackenzie dominated the school for well over thirty years. Corder was a book collector, a member of the recently formed folklore research society, and a romantic; he was anything but a martinet.

In his 1979 study of British music at this period, Peter J. Pirie comments:

> Corder's only student of considerable talent was Arnold Bax (1883-1953). The bulk of the really talented pupils went to the College and Stanford: in those years he taught Vaughan Williams, Gustav Holst, John Ireland (1879-1962) and Frank Bridge (1879-1941) among others. However, examining all the facts, and weighing his pupils' reactions to him, it is hard to resist the conclusion that Stanford's legendary reputation as a teacher has been exaggerated.[2]

Pirie says of Edmund Jenkins's teacher:

> Corder was mildly progressive, and so permissive a teacher that he also left his mark on his pupils; but a very different mark from that left by Stanford. All his pupils lacked discipline, and even Arnold Bax was slow in finding direction.[3]

Bax had studied under Corder twelve years before Jenkins, and the Royal Academy of Music at that time is described by Bax's biographer as being an institution that trembled under the principalship of Sir Alexander Campbell Mackenzie, a fiery Scot whose outspoken criticism of modernist tendencies in the work of his students was belied by his liberal-minded policies for their musical education. It was to his enlightened thinking that many young musicians owed their first appreciation and understanding of the late works of Liszt.[4]

Corder's influence was "a permissive rather than a restricting influence."[5] His obituary in the *Times* in 1932 described Corder as "a man of emotional and somewhat melancholy temperament" whose musical tastes were first Wagner and then Dvořák.[6] An American commented that Corder "was remarkably successful as a teacher, many prominent British composers having been his pupils."[7]

Students at the Royal Academy of Music could study various instruments; Edmund Jenkins was one of the few to choose clarinet. He was taught by Edward J. Augarde, who had been a pupil at the academy, where he had been awarded the wind instrument Ross Scholarship for 1910. Jenkins also studied the piano under Morton and French language with Henri Bosc. The files of the Royal Academy of Music indicate that Jenkins paid his application fee on September 14, and recorded his home address as 20 Franklin Street, Charleston, S.C., U.S.A.; his date and place of birth as April 9, 1894, at Charleston, S.C.; and indicate that his father had supplied him with sufficient funds to pay his way, for the entry against "Guarantor's Name, Address" reads "self." The clarinet and French lessons cost extra, the term's fourteen guineas paying for composition and piano instruction only. The balance was recorded on September 23. Jenkins was paying the academy about the same as his father had proposed to pay Eugene Mikell for the U.S. tour.

Few foreign students were enrolled at the academy, according to its records and the memories of students of the period. When they were from outside the British Isles they were from the colonies or Empire—Canada, Hong Kong, South Africa. There was a cosmopolitan atmosphere created by the Ashkenazi Jews whose parents had fled czarist pogroms in eastern Europe to settle in Britain, and a few others from exotic backgrounds, including Jean Pougnet from the Indian Ocean island of Mauritius, who required private English lessons to understand the instruction.[8] Giovanni Barbirolli, of French and Italian parentage, was born in London but spoke English as his third language. Known to his fellow students as "Tito" but later to achieve fame in Britain and America as Sir John Barbirolli, young Barbirolli was a member of the student orchestra at a concert given on December 11, 1914, at the Queen's Hall.

Concerts were held every two weeks at the academy, either in the Duke's Hall, on the eastern side of the college, or at the Queen's Hall in Langham Place, ten minutes walk away. This routine was interrupted by the war from time to time. The Queen's Hall had been built in 1893 and had been used for the annual summer Promenade Concerts from 1895. It was London's premier concert hall, and it had among the finest acoustics in the world. It seated nearly twenty-five hundred, had seventeen exits (meeting the most modern fire regulations), and had a level floor, which was below street level. Chamber music lovers were considered when Knightley designed the building, and a smaller hall, seating five hundred, was in the roof, which was a few steps above street level due to the unorthodox sunken main hall.

The platform of the Queen's Hall could hold four hundred musicians, but the students of the academy numbered about one hundred when at three o'clock in the afternoon of Friday, December 11, 1914, they presented ten items, four written by former students. Adah Rogalsky sang Corder's *Fear Not the Wind or the Wave;* and Winifred Small performed two violin pieces from Mackenzie's Opus 32; Edward German's *Spring* from *The Seasons* was played by the orchestra, which included Jenkins and two other clarinetists. Jenkins's professor Edward Augarde played an item by Eric Grant, which was preceded by David Harry singing *Onaway: Awake, Beloved,* from Coleridge-Taylor's *Hiawatha.*

The school shut for a three-week break for Christmas and the New Year, opening for the Lent term on January 7, 1915. The office staff was active before the teaching staff, and Jenkins's fourteen guineas are noted on the file on January 5. He ceased paying for French lessons, which suggests that his education at Avery was sufficient, although language studies, usually in Italian, were essential for pupils specializing in singing.

The next musical event that involved Edmund Jenkins that has been traced was another afternoon concert by the students at the

Queen's Hall on Friday, February 26. Jenkins and Augarde were the clarinet section when the orchestra presented eight items, including Weber's Opus 75, Verdi's aria *Ritorna Vincitor* from *Aïda*, and the first movement of Brahms's Piano Concerto in D.

Edmund Jenkins was probably living at 181 or 99 Brondesbury Park in northwest London in March 1915, when he received a letter from Stella in Teignmouth, Devon. Stella noted that "my sister anticipates seeing you when she comes to London," and "I believe you said you would be examined before the end of the month. Well! I wish you the best of luck." Brondesbury Park was a pleasant suburban street of substantial houses just six stops on the railway from Baker Street, five minutes from York Gate.

The examination was a success, for the file is annotated "Bronze Medal S. Sing," indicating that Edmund Jenkins's singing studies with Harreld in Atlanta had given him a higher standard than many at London's Royal Academy of Music. The entry is made opposite that of May 5, 1915, which also shows that he was paying for singing lessons that continued until the end of 1915.

The Duke's Hall at York Gate was one of several chamber music concert halls in London, but it was used mainly for academy events rather than commercial concerts. On Tuesday, June 29, 1915, Jenkins, Barbirolli, and Winifred Small, with fellow students and teachers, were under the baton of Sir Alexander Mackenzie as usual. Fifteen items were presented, including works by Gounod, Handel, César Franck, Meyerbeer, Saint-Saëns, and Coleridge-Taylor, whose *Hiawatha's Vision* was sung by Richard Tregoning.

The first academic year ended on July 24, 1915, and Jenkins had two months vacation. By this time he knew that he had won an orchestral scholarship, which paid his basic tuition fees. He still had to find his daily living expenses, pay for sheet music, instruments, and lodgings. Good sight-reading musicians had many opportunities for work in the restaurants, cafés, clubs, and theaters that provided entertainment in London during the war years, and it is almost certain that Edmund Jenkins joined his fellow students in such activities. The need for good musicians had been mentioned in the Chicago *Defender*, one of the leading black newspapers in the United States. On May 22, 1915, it reported "Joe Jordan plays in London cafe. Race musicians being called from America to take place of Germans in London hotels and cafes. They are there as entertainers in hotels and cafes in London and summer resorts." Earlier, the New York *Age* of March 11, 1915, had reported that the Clef Club had organized seven musicians to Britain that month, led by Dan Kildaire.[9]

One of the many black groups working in Britain before war had broken out was The Versatile Three, which had included Anthony Tuck, Charles Mills, and Gus Haston. On April 8, 1915, the New York *Age* reported, "Rehearsals are being held under the direction of Will Marion Cook for the presentation of a big colored orchestra that will be sent on at the Alhambra in London for two months. Gus Haston, who is back in London, is engineering the deal."

Pit bands in theaters, small orchestras in restaurants, and various musical groups in cafés, music halls, at "silent" movies, and at private and public dances, gave plenty of employment to musicians. In addition there were the classical music concerts, rehearsals, and private lessons of the schooled musician. Any leader would have welcomed Jenkins, who was able to play the violin, the clarinet, the piano, and all the brass instruments of his father's band, including the cornet, the trombone, and the various horns. Extra entertainments were arranged for battle-weary troops, wealthy industrialists, and for workers benefiting from high wages and steady work in war industries. Barbirolli joined the pit band at The Duke of York's Theater, and later claimed to have played in every theater built in London before 1923.[10] He was paid five pounds ($25) for the eight performances at The Duke of York's, and less for the "tea time music" that he played with a group that was to include fellow 'cellist Bram Martin, later a dance band leader.[11]

Edmund Jenkins's nonacademic work was described in an American magazine published in 1925. "He also did a great deal of work in theatrical orchestras in London and the provinces of Great Britain. Chief among these periods with theaters is the season spent as first clarinetist at the Savoy Theater as well as the holding of the same chair at the Grand Theater in Llandudno, Wales."[12]

Jenkins also attended concerts and recitals, for the race restrictions of Atlanta were not found in Britain. He kept the program of one such London concert given by the Royal Choral Society at the Royal Albert Hall, a venue notorious for its poor acoustics but nevertheless a major concert and public hall. The concert, given on February 6, 1915, was of scenes from Coleridge-Taylor's *Hiawatha*, and the orchestra included Augarde (bass clarinet), academy trumpet tutor John Solomon, and A. E. Brain (horn), later a member of the Queen's Hall Orchestra. One of the three trombonists was Jesse Stamp, later a close associate of Edmund.

Following some summer activities, which have not been traced, Edmund Jenkins returned to the academy to begin his second year of studies under Frederick Corder in the term beginning on September 23, 1915. Jenkins's scholarship was for two years. Continuing with his piano and clarinet studies, he took extra lessons in singing for the Michaelmas term only. The only concert featuring Jenkins that term was at the Duke's Hall on November 4. The sixteen-year-old Barbirolli, no longer "Master" but "Mr.," was a member of a quartet playing two pieces by Brahms. Winifred Small duetted with Leo Livens in two *allegretti* by César Franck. The concert began with a string quartet by Dvořák, and included Beethoven's *andante* and *rondo* for piano, oboe, clarinet, horn, and bassoon, in which Jenkins played the clarinet.

In the Lent term following the Christmas vacation, Jenkins ceased his singing lessons, but continued with composition, piano, and clarinet. On Monday, February 21, 1916, under the direction of Mackenzie at the Duke's Hall the students presented another concert. The final item was Saint-Saëns's *Caprice*, Opus 79, for flute, oboe, clarinet, and piano. Doris Griffiths played the flute; Lucy Vincent played the oboe; Jenkins the clarinet; and the piano was played by Arthur Sandford. All three students were closely associated with Jenkins during his years at the academy. Sandford was a brilliant pianist, who won the Mendelssohn Prize and is one of the few students mentioned by Corder in his 1922 privately published history of the Royal Academy of Music.[13] Sandford's musical career was checkered mainly by personal problems, but musicians who knew him remarked that he was an excellent accompanist and superb pianist, and was always employed by the academy when he was free to rejoin their staff.

The academy had between seven and eight hundred students, and discipline was relaxed. Tutors such as Augarde who were not required every day would take other teaching posts, and play and tour with orchestras. While away from York Gate they would arrange a substitute teacher, or give more lessons at a later date in order to keep their part of the contract. Students were also able to take time off for concert tours and other musical events. It cannot be certain, therefore, that Jenkins was in London during the weekend of the Saint-Saëns concert or that he took part in the entertainment of some wounded soldiers who had been invited to tea at York Gate on Saturday, February 19, when the students gave a "Ragtime Class."

At another Duke's Hall concert, on Monday, May 29, 1916, Jenkins and his three colleagues Griffiths, Vincent, and Sandford, presented a three-movement suite by Amberg as the first item of a concert that included works by Elgar, Puccini, and Beethoven. Fellow students, parents, friends, and members of staff were the audience at these concerts, although the public was free to attend.

At the end of the term a grand concert was given by the students and staff at the Queen's Hall, and at the concert of June 27, 1916, Jenkins and Augarde were the clarinet section, and Bizet, Beethoven, and Tchaikovsky were among the composers whose works were performed. Jenkins's abilities on the clarinet were recognized by the award of a bronze medal, which is noted on his file on July 10, 1916. After two years of studies he had won two medals and a scholarship. His work with Corder had attracted some attention, for the academy magazine, which was produced for and by the students, noted that Jenkins had composed "a new overture 'Much Ado' written for the occasion by a student, Edmund T. Jenkins" for a June performance of the academy's dramatic class, which presented Shakespeare's *Much Ado About Nothing*.[14] The student journalist made no critical comment, but an independent weekly musical magazine did review the event, commenting:

> The orchestra played some very interesting music during the evening, under the direction of Mr. Frederick Corder, including a new Overture, "Much Ado", written for the occasion by a student, Edmund T. Jenkins. Though not strikingly original in design or treatment, the Overture indicated an engaging knowledge of orchestral effect which should carry the student far. It was splendidly played, and the composer had an enthusiastic call.[15]

Edmund Jenkins left London in the summer of 1916 and went 230 miles to north Wales, where he met William Hughes, the former missionary to the Congo who had known Paul "Gabasie" Daniels nearly twenty years before.

CHAPTER 7

HIS EFFORT WAS FULL OF PROMISE

Edmund Jenkins played in the theater orchestra at the Grand Theater, Llandudno, during the summer season of 1916. Llandudno was a resort town of ten thousand inhabitants, described in a contemporary account as a "lively, progressive and popular watering place."[1] Tourists from London could travel there by train in four and a half hours, and slower rail links connected it to the industrial cotton towns of Lancashire and the port of Liverpool, which also had a regular steamer connection. Llandudno had a wide stretch of beach, a backdrop of the Welsh mountains, spectacular cliffs on the headland called the Great Orme, and a gracious townscape developed since the 1850s. It was Welsh enough to be "foreign"—Welsh was spoken in the streets by the majority of the inhabitants—but not alarmingly so. It was an ideal vacation center, and the town offered motor excursions to the mountains, including the Swallow Falls at the beauty spot of Betws-y-Coed, which were visited by Edmund Jenkins.[2]

The considerable numbers of holiday makers in the town were offered a variety of entertainments. The pier, where the Liverpool steamers docked, attracted day excursionists, and the nearby Pier Theater had an orchestra of over twenty musicians, well known in Britain. There was a cinema, a bandstand, other theaters, and "Nigger Minstrels" on the beach.

In early 1916 the government had introduced conscription, having relied on volunteers for eighteen months. Theater managers and orchestra leaders sought elderly musicians, who were unlikely to be drafted, or foreigners, especially neutrals such as Americans. This gave greater opportunities to the twenty-two-year-old Edmund Jenkins. Although wartime regulations in Britain required aliens to register with the police whatever their locality, whether temporary or permanent, Jenkins seems to have had no problem in joining the orchestra at Llandudno's Grand Theater when it opened for the summer season on Monday, July 17, 1916.[3]

The Grand Theater had opened in 1901 on a site a little out of the center of town. As many as 730 patrons could watch the shows, which were usually touring companies playing for three performances and then moving on. A. G. Pugh, the manager, failed to get the free publicity that the Pier Theater got in the local newspapers, but the Grand offered items such as *Charley's Aunt, Tantalizing Tommy, The Belle of New York*, and *Peg O' My Heart*, all London successes. Two shows were held on Saturday.

William Hughes's black training school in Colwyn Bay had collapsed in 1912 when he lost his case against the superb lawyer, politician, and rogue[4] Horatio Bottomley whose *John Bull* magazine had publicized a scandal in December 1911.[5] The supporters in the chapels and churches of Wales ceased their subscriptions and Hughes was declared a bankrupt. By 1916 Hughes had recovered and had returned to live in the Congo Institute building in Colwyn Bay's Nant-y-Glyn Road, six miles by tram from Llandudno.[6] Edmund Jenkins visited Hughes, and kept a four-page pamphlet that Hughes had printed, telling of the capture of the German African colony of Cameroon, and the requirements of the ex-Institute evangelists who were still active in Christian work in that country. Hughes probably told Edmund Jenkins of the achievements of some of his former pupils, such as Davidson Don Jabavu from south Africa, who had studied at Colwyn Bay from 1903, completing his degree in London in 1912. Jabavu may have been known to Jenkins from his visit to Tuskegee, Alabama, or from his participation with his father John Tengo Jabavu at the 1911 London Universal Races Congress that had attracted much American support, including that of W. E. B. Du Bois, and Booker T. Washington's secretary Robert Moton.[7] Jenkins's conversations with Hughes would have reinforced the opinions he heard expressed by Paul Daniels and Parson Jenkins after their British experiences.

The season at the Grand Theater ended in late September, but Edmund Jenkins's late return to York Gate would not have led to any disciplinary action, particularly since the staff was reduced due to military service and administration was a little chaotic.[8] Edmund Jenkins joined Arthur Sandford to present piano duets at the dramatic class on November 30 and December 1, 1916. The three pieces included the last movement of Mackenzie's *Scottish Rhapsody no. 2.* The weekly *Musical News* reviewed the second performance:

> An interesting programme of music for two pianos was submitted by Messrs. Arthur L. Sandford and Edmund T. Jenkins, who were very much of one mind in their duets, which were rendered with wonderful precision and smoothness of execution. Their music contributed greatly to a very enjoyable evening.[9]

Not all programs of events at the academy have survived the years, but Jenkins kept the program of the Duke's Hall performances of December 12 and 13, 1916, which included Corder's operetta *Margaret: The Blind Girl of Castél Cuillé* which, like Coleridge-Taylor's operetta of the same title, was based on Longfellow's poem. On Friday, December 15, the end-of-term students' concert presented works by Grieg, Bizet, Saint-Saëns, Puccini, Meyerbeer, and Paderewski. The orchestra included Augarde and Jenkins, Barbirolli, and Winifred Small, who had been assisting with the teaching at the academy and was subprofessor, ensemble playing. Sandford had written an overture entitled *Rustic,* which was played by the orchestra, and Adah Rogalsky sang *Love's Hour,* which had been written by Jenkins. The critic of the *Musical News* was present, commenting "Miss Adah Rogalsky, the possessor of a good voice, introduced a pleasing MS [manuscript, i.e., unpublished] song by Edmund T. Jenkins (scholar)."[10]

The lyrics had been written by William Archer Plowright, who was to be associated with Jenkins for the next four years. He was a water colorist, poet, illustrator, and Victorian man of taste. He had written lyrics for Sir Arthur Sullivan, and occasionally published articles in the local newspaper in northwest London's Cricklewood, a railway suburb.[11] Active in the local Congregational church, and writing for the railway workers club, Plowright had achieved some local fame when his dog fell from Cricklewood railway platform in front of the London-Scotland express, to emerge unharmed.[12]

The chaos in the administration at York Gate is evidenced by the lack of a tick in the "Principal Study—Composition" column of Jenkins's file for the Lent and midsummer terms of 1917, for it is very doubtful that Corder did not teach Jenkins for two terms in 1917.

On February 19, 1917, Jenkins joined Sandford and Doris Griffiths to play Saint-Saëns's *Tarantelle* for flute, clarinet, and piano, Opus 6, at the Duke's Hall. On March 27 the orchestral concert at the Queen's Hall under Mackenzie involved works by Liszt, Weber, Purcell, and Grieg as well as a song by Debussy and another collaboration of Jenkins and Plowright. Augarde and Jenkins were in the orchestra and Plowright in the audience when Marjorie Perkins sang their *How Sweet Is Life*. The *Musical News* of March 31, 1917, reviewed the concert.

> A song, "How Sweet Is Life" by a student, Mr. Edmund T. Jenkins, who is a native of Africa, showed the composer to be possessed of a vein of melody, not original as yet, and of a style which needs unifying, but his effort was full of promise, especially in the matter of orchestration. The song was well rendered by Miss Marjorie Perkins.

Edmund Jenkins had made sufficient progress after two and a half years at the Royal Academy of Music for his compositions to be performed at London's leading concert hall in a program of music by European masters. Anti-German feelings had discouraged the public performance of works by the German composers, but Corder's lifelong enthusiasm for Wagner would have encouraged discussion of the master's work with Jenkins.

More recognition of Jenkins's skills is found in the annotation of May 24, 1917, in the academy files which says "Bronze medal Piano Silver medal Clarinet & S.Sing." One month later on June 22 Jenkins's composition for grand organ and orchestra entitled *Prélude Réligieuse* was performed at the Queen's Hall. The critic of the *Musical News* of June 30, 1917, noted that "A Prélude Réligieuse for orchestra and organ by Edmund T. Jenkins was of an appropriately dignified character." The academy files do not show the name of the organist but do indicate that Jenkins and Augarde were the clarinet players as usual. Jenkins had not studied the organ at the academy; this work shows the instrumental skills he had obtained in America.

On July 9 at the Duke's Hall three pieces by the British composer Hamilton Harty were presented by Lucy Vincent (oboe) and Edmund Jenkins (piano), whose performance was described in the *Musical News* of July 14, 1917, merely as "neatly played." Sandford had one of his compositions played by Leslie England, and Gladys Chester played two of Mackenzie's violin works. Gladys Chester and her brother Russell were two of the academy pupils who were to be close friends with Edmund Jenkins.

Jenkins's scholarship was renewed for another year, but Jenkins ceased studying the piano from the summer of 1917. In 1917 Edmund Jenkins met two West Indian students in London. Their friendship was deep, and shows something of the black community in Britain in which Edmund Jenkins was to play an important part.

CHAPTER 8

THE ART OF PRIZE WINNING

Blacks had resided in Britain before Carolina was settled by the British. Although the rise of other industrial nations had reduced Britain's trading influence, London was the largest and most populated city in the world, King George V was monarch of one-quarter of the world's inhabitants, and Britain exerted a great deal of influence in the black world. Educational facilities in Africa and the Caribbean were limited, and black students traveled to Britain for training. The medical schools in Edinburgh attracted many blacks, including Theophilus Scholes from Jamaica, Ishmael Pratt from Sierra Leone, and Wilson Mongoli Sebeta from south Africa's Basutoland, all associated with Colwyn Bay's Institute.[1] One of Edmund Jenkins's black London friends had attended Edinburgh University's medical school, and, like Jenkins, was to be involved in black politics in Britain in the 1920s.

John Alcindor was twenty years old when he traveled on a scholarship from Trinidad in 1893 to study medicine in Edinburgh. He qualified in 1899, and in the summer of 1900 joined Frederick Loudin and Samuel Coleridge-Taylor at a race conference organized by the Trinidad-born lawyer Henry Sylvester Williams and the Atlanta-based W. E. B. Du Bois. Alcindor worked in London from 1899. Another black at the 1900 London race conference was the Liverpool-born John Richard Archer, whose father was from Barbados. Archer and Williams were successful candidates in the municipal elections in London in November 1906, and Archer had been selected by his fellow councilors in 1913 to become mayor of Battersea,[2] which was reported in the black press in the United States and would have been known to Parson Jenkins. Williams had returned to Trinidad by 1908 (after a career that had taken him to Cape Town) where he worked with the part-Chinese, part-black lawyer Eugene Bernard Acham-Chen,[3] whose son Percy was a law student in London and a friend of Edmund Jenkins.

Archer and Alcindor were friends of Jenkins, as was another Trinidad black, Felix Eugene Michael Hercules, who had been in London since 1914.[4] A friend of Hercules, and a good friend of Jenkins, was Randall H. Lockhart. Lockhart was born in Martinique in the French West Indies, and arrived in London before the war with his father. He studied at Clapham College in south London, returned to Martinique, and then back to London, where he was a medical student at King's College for some months. He changed to law because he liked to argue. He met Jenkins by 1917 and through Jenkins met Barbirolli. Lockhart recalled the musicians' friendship in 1979: "They were fond of each other and my impression was that each respected the other's talent."[5]

Another Caribbean black friend of Jenkins was Harold R. D. Piper, who was a few days younger than Edmund. Born in Montserrat, Piper spent most of his life in Trinidad. He also had met Jenkins in London by 1917, and their friendship developed, and led them to share accommodations, sometimes with a medical student from Trinidad, the part-Chinese, part-black Felix Hiram "Harry" Leekam. Leekam was joined in London by his younger brother Freddy or Ferdie, also a medical student, who joined the group. Harry Leekam remained in London after he qualified at St. Mary's Hospital. Alcindor was one of four District Medical Officers in Paddington, operated his own practice in the Harrow Road, ten minutes from St. Mary's Hospital, and was active in the Red Cross. Harold Moody, from Jamaica, had his own practice in south London's Camberwell, which enabled him to sponsor some of his relatives from Jamaica to study in Britain. Aston Moody added a British dentistry qualification to those obtained in Pennsylvania, and another brother, Ludlow, was studying medicine in London when he met Jenkins.

Women in the group included Trinidad-born Audrey Jeffers who lived in north London's Finchley Road area. Lockhart recalled

Audrey Jeffers in a letter dated August 26, 1979: "She was one of our band of friends, but rather on the fringe due to her being a woman. Not that any of us were prejudiced against the sex—far from it—but a woman does not so readily fit in a bohemian company."

Audrey Jeffers associated in London with Muriel Barbour-James, who later helped her in her social work in Trinidad. John Alexander Barbour-James, Muriel's father, may have been the catalyst for this group of blacks in London. Born in British Guiana in 1867, Barbour-James had been involved in black affairs in Guiana in the 1890s. He was a postal official in that colony, transferring to west Africa in the middle of 1902. His wife and family did not make the journey to the Gold Coast, where Barbour-James spent much of his time traveling, inspecting the postal services in the colony. His family settled in Acton, west London, where they were joined by Barbour-James on his regular and lengthy leaves. Three of his children were born in Britain. Their home was a regular center for black people visiting Britain, and Barbour-James kept up his links with the Caribbean and Africa after he had retired in 1917. His children were musical. During his Guiana days Barbour-James had known a black headmaster named David Mitchell; Mitchell's son Lionel was studying law in London, and was an active associate of Jenkins, Lockhart, Piper, and Leekam.

Barbour-James's best friend was the Gold Coast merchant Robert Broadhurst, who had lived in England for some years, and was a friend of Archer, Alcindor, and Edmund Jenkins. Barbour-James had seen the increasing racial horrors of the United States and had organized pleas to American presidents as early as 1902.[6] His compassion led him to be a founder of the comforts fund for British West Indian troops on active service in France during the war years, which may have been the activity that brought the group of blacks in London together. Broadhurst's links with the aged Liberian patriot Edward Blyden in Britain in 1901, the activities of the African supporters of the Congo Institute, and the race conferences held in Britain from 1900 suggest, however, a greater amount of black activity in Britain than previous writings would indicate.

The United States entered into the war in 1917. At the beginning of the year a group of five white musicians from New Orleans, who had been attracting crowds at a New York dance restaurant, had recorded for two American record companies. The records of this Original Dixieland Jazz Band (ODJB) brought jazz to Britain, changed musical attitudes, and gave opportunities to Edmund Jenkins.

Jenkins started his fourth year at the Royal Academy of Music in September 1917. His main study was composition with Corder, but in place of the piano lessons he studied the organ with H. W. Richards, and his clarinet tutor was now Herbert Stuteley. Augarde appears to have been absent from London, for Jenkins was principal clarinet at the Queen's Hall concert of December 11, 1917. Three of Jenkins's songs were presented, *Doubting, The Fiddler's Fiddle,* and *A Romance.*

Jenkins, Sandford, and the two Chesters were actively associating that fall, for the academy magazine in November 1917 reported, "Under the auspices of Branch B, a new journal run by students, with Mr. Edmund Jenkins as editor, under the title of the 'Academite', is to make its appearance. Copies, 6½d each, can be had on application to Mr. Russell Chester, at the Academy."[7] The first issue sold 250 copies, but the magazine collapsed the year after Jenkins left York Gate.

The war was having an effect on the academy, with reduced office staff, more female students than usual, interrupted instruction as tutors and students were enlisted, and the trauma of hearing the regular announcement of death, injury, or imprisonment of former pupils. London continued to be bombed by airship and later airplane, and one of the eight hundred bombs that fell on the capital hit the Queen's Hall. Bomb attacks on the city killed 522 people. The paper shortage made the *Musical News* appear every two weeks.

In late 1917 Jenkins was awarded the Oliveira Prescott Gift, a prize of books and music, for his achievements in composition. Jenkins was living at 149 Sumatra Road, in London's West Hampstead, on December 22 when the secretary of the National Orchestral Association responded to his letter of December 20 by accepting his resignation from this professional association which had banned members from "accepting engagements at the Marlborough Theatre under present conditions." The Marlborough Theatre was a two-thousand-seat theater in north London's Holloway, usually showing plays from London's "West End" theatrical district.

Black American troops entered France in 1918. The 15th New York Infantry Regiment included James Reese Europe and Francis Eugene Mikell, who was responsible for the band. The twenty-eight official musicians were augmented by sixteen soldiers who were the pride of black New York. Extra funds had been collected to encourage top quality black musicians to join the Regiment, whose arrangements of American popular songs brought the sound of live jazz to Europe. Three of the musicians were from the Jenkins Orphanage. Attached to the French army, and renumbered 369 Regiment, this black unit had an honored fighting record in eastern France.[8] It had trained in Spartanburg, S.C., and had been insulted by white Americans. Other black regiments were in France, including the 807 Pioneer Infantry, whose band was led by Bert Williams's associate Will Vodery.[9]

The soldiers of the British West Indies Regiment served in Belgium and France and were given leave in London. The group of black students, including Jenkins, Piper, and Jeffers, befriended them, taking them to the house of a Trinidad family named Iles, at 24 Goldhurst Terrace, a few minutes walk from Sumatra Road. Parties, and other semiformal gatherings, took place at the Iles's home, and Jenkins played the piano there.

Two chamber concerts were given by the academy in Lent term, 1918, on February 18 and March 6, a production of Arthur Sanford's opera *The Lover from Japan* on March 14 and 16, and the usual concert at the Queen's Hall, on March 22, when Gladys Chester played Jenkins's violin piece *Romance*. This summary of the term's events was detailed in issue 3 of *The Academite*, which was published for the midsummer term, 1918. Jenkins's organ studies with H. W. Richards continued through the Lent and midsummer terms of 1918, as well as his clarinet with Stutely and his composition with Corder, but from January 1918 he began a study of harmony under Percy Miles. His file records, on May 16, 1918, the award of the Charles Lucas Prize, which was named in honor of the academy professor who had taught Mackenzie. First awarded in 1875, it was another sign of Jenkins's merit, and, coming so soon after the Prescott prize, was probably the clue to the humorous question in *The Academite*, "Guess which student was recently requested to write an article on the 'Art of Prize-winning'?" for there were only forty prizes at York Gate.

Jenkins did write an article for that edition of the student magazine, entitled *The Man Who Knew Beethoven*, which ended "I know Beethoven, the baker, well; he lives in Water Street!" The magazine also announced that the RAM Tennis Club, which had courts at Grove End Road in Hampstead, would start on May 31, 1918, and that Jenkins was the manager.

In September 1918 Edmund Jenkins started his fifth year at the Royal Academy of Music, for his Orchestral Scholarship had been extended again. He no longer took clarinet lessons, but gave them instead. Jenkins's name appears in the academy prospectus for the three academic years from September 1918, but he taught only for the year ending July 1919. His pupil was seventeen-year-old Anita Harrison from South Shields in the northeast of England. Her principal study was the piano, and she also had instruction in harmony. From September 1919 her clarinet lessons were given by Augarde, and she left the academy after the usual four years, with one prize, one certificate, and two medals for her piano skills. She married a Swede in 1925 and had an active career as a concert pianist in Scandinavia. Her daughter advised in March 1980 that she knew "that my mother learnt to play the clarinet and that she had a coloured teacher. I did not know his name before—I just remember my mother telling me that her teacher was a Negro. My mother was a pianist, and she just had to learn a second instrument at the Academy, and she chose the clarinet."[10]

Mackenzie had given Jenkins a letter dated September 20, 1918, which confirmed that he had been a student since September 1914 and that he had "developed a considerable gift for musical composition during his stay with us. We wish him every success, as we think him possessed of a distinct talent for music." This may not mean a great deal, as he gave similar reports to everybody, according to one veteran.[11]

Jenkins and the other members of Branch B gave a dance on November 5, 1918, and "about 150 students and friends were present."[12] The warfare came to an end on November 11, 1918, after the armistice was signed, and, following a chamber concert, a fancy dress dance was held on November 20, attracting over 450 people. It was at such an event, or at the concerts, that Jenkins met Winifred Small's parents, who asked him to tea at their north London home. Jenkins went there at least twice. Jenkins had not been

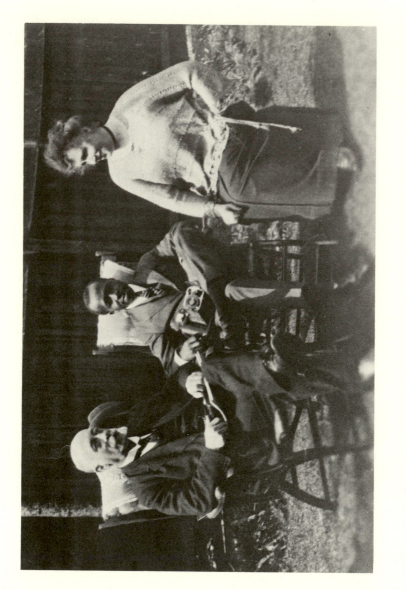

4. Edmund Jenkins with Winifred Small's parents, Palmers' Green, north London, ca. 1920. *Courtesy the late Winifred Small of London.*

well during 1918, but he was appearing at the Royal Academy's events, for *The Academite* no. 5 of Lent term, 1919, included another series of "Guess Who's" including "Guess who speaks the American lingo as if to the manner born."

The same year that Jenkins was teaching Miss Harrison he received two more acknowledgments of his skills. In late 1918 he won a certificate for clarinet and sight reading, and in February 1919 he was awarded the Battison Haynes Prize. This was a cash prize, previously won by Bax, in 1902.

Celebration of the peace by their huge fancy dress party was not the only activity of the students, who had formed concert parties to entertain the Allied troops in France, and, on Friday afternoon, December 13, 1918, entertained 150 wounded soldiers from "the Overseas Dominions and the United States" at the Duke's Hall, followed by tea.[13] The end of the fighting was the beginning of debate on the new world order, and the fall of 1918 involved many of Jenkins's black friends in political moves which were to involve him.

CHAPTER 9

THE COTERIE OF FRIENDS

Benjamin Brawley had written to Jenkins in 1916, suggesting that they cooperate to produce a cantata on the biblical story of the seven sleepers of Ephesus.[1] This story had particular appeal for black Americans who could identify with the seven persecuted Christians whose awakening found Christianity triumphant. From his American friends and British newspaper reports Jenkins would have known of the growing racial bitterness in America, the work of Du Bois and the National Association for the Advancement of Colored People (NAACP), and the prejudice of Woodrow Wilson's administration. The years of warfare had increased expectation of fairer opportunities and the old order had been questioned by the overthrow of the Imperial Russian regime, the growth of socialism, trade unions, and women's rights organizations.

In October and November 1918 Jenkins's friends were involved in a series of meetings at London's Cannon Street Hotel, and, later, at the Great Eastern Hotel. Reports in the London press list some of the sixty-odd people present at the Great Eastern Hotel on December 18, 1918, when many of Jenkins's black friends formed the African Progress Union (APU), which had been established "to promote the general welfare of Africans and Afro-peoples" and to create "a public sentiment in favour of brotherhood in its broadest sense."[2] Jenkins must have known of this group, even if he was not present, for he was later to be a committee member. John Archer said that "the Peace Conference should contain a proposal for the better treatment of the coloured races, and for greater facilities for educational advancement. If they were good enough to fight the wars of the country, they were good enough to receive the benefits of the country."[3] Archer, a former mayor of Battersea (he was still a councilor) and Broadhurst, the Gold Coast merchant, seem to have been the main activists behind the APU, and their names appeared on the APU's correspondence with the British government, requesting that an African should be seconded to the British delegation at the discussion that had to follow the cease fire of November 11, 1918.[4] Broadhurst had earlier signed a lengthy telegram to Prime Minister Lloyd George, conveying the APU's plea that the ex-German colonies in Africa should have civilian rulers as soon as possible, and also that they should not be returned to Germany.[5]

Felix Hercules, K. F. Tandoh of the Gold Coast, and E. P. Bruyning from British Guiana were the other officials of the APU. John Barbour-James and his daughter Muriel were present, and so were their friends Audrey Jeffers, Alfred Adderley from the Bahamas, John Eldred Taylor, and Sylvia Acham-Chen, all associates of Jenkins.[6] The Sierra Leone Taylor had been producing a monthly magazine, *The African Telegraph*, which Jenkins would have read. Jenkins would also have known Archer's involvement in the election campaign of the radical, socialist, and feminist Charlotte Despard that December, for Lloyd George had called a parliamentary election. The changes in British society at this period are seen in the large increase in the electorate, due to abolishment of male property requirements and the extension of the vote to women over thirty years of age. Despard's prewar suffrage work had involved Mrs. Anne Cobden-Sanderson, the daughter of the great Victorian radical Richard Cobden. Her sister Jane attended the APU meeting with her publisher husband Thomas Fisher Unwin, a direct link with the 1900 race conference; Jane Cobden Unwin and Despard's painter friend Felix Moscheles had both been involved with Archer at Henry Sylvester Williams's Pan-African Conference. The radical dissenter element in British society had aided the south African black nationalist Sol Plaatje who had been in England from 1914 until 1917; Plaatje was well known in the Brotherhood Movement during the war years, and had published, in May 1916, a book protesting the 1913 white takeover of most of the land in southern

Africa. Jenkins and his friends would have read Plaatje's *Native Life in South Africa*.

Other friends of Jenkins at the APU meeting included Edmund Fitzgerald Fredericks from British Guiana; Alphonso Luke from Trinidad; Thomas Hutton-Mills, J. E. Hutton-Mills, and A. G. Heward Mills, three brothers from the Gold Coast; the part-Sudanese part-Egyptian Dusé Mohammed Ali, who had been publishing *The African Times and Orient Review* in London since 1912; Dolly Durham from the Caribbean; Miss C. Amado Taylor, a nurse and midwife from Sierra Leone; and S. A. Hughes, a university student also from Sierra Leone. There were musicians in the group at the dinner party at the Great Eastern, including Frank Lacton and L. Wendell Bruce James, who played the piano to songs by Jeffers, Adderley, and a West Indian, Mr. L. Drysdale. Bruce James was a West Indian friend of one of John Barbour-James's student sons.[7]

In the United States Benjamin Brawley had been busy working on several books. He wrote to his friend and old pupil Jenkins from Morehouse College on December 7, 1918, telling him of the changes that had taken place because of the war, including college students in uniform and regular drill. He told Jenkins that his book *The Negro in Literature and Art* had been published in March 1918, followed in June by *Your Negro Neighbor*. He had edited a school book entitled *New Era Declamations* and had mailed a copy to Jenkins in London. He was arranging with his publishers to print his "rather vigorous little book *Africa And The War*," which was due to be released on January 1, 1919. Brawley was not the only black anxious to press the black cause, for Barbour-James had given a lecture concert in the second week of December 1918 to promote the finance of a book detailing African contributions to the war.[8] Booker T. Washington's former secretary Emmett J. Scott was working on his history of the black American contribution to the war, which was published in 1919. Washington's successor at Tuskegee Institute, Robert Moton, had been seconded to the U.S. peace negotiations, which was known to Broadhurst and Archer of the APU by December 23, indicating the American links to the London blacks.[9]

Little is known of the concerts and recitals of the Royal Academy of Music from surviving documents at York Gate after early 1919.

Jenkins's Battison Haynes Prize, awarded in February 1919, was for his slow movement and *rondo* for four wind instruments and piano.[10] This was played at a students' chamber concert on March 5, 1919, and reviewed by Herbert Nelson in the *Musical News* of March 15, 1919, who mentioned other items "and the Slow Movement and Rondo from a Quintet for Flute, two Clarinets, Horn, and Pianoforte, by Edmund T. Jenkins, a scholar, a work which shows promising marks of originality and which was neatly played by the composer, together with Mary Underwood, G. Stutely, Francis Bradley, and Marjorie Herman."

Jenkins was the clarinetist at a concert at the Queen's Hall on March 27, 1919, but the program is unknown. The April 1919 issue of *RAM Club Magazine* announced Jenkins's prize, which would have been handed to him at the prize giving on July 18, 1919, at the Central Hall, Westminster, by Lady Dewar. The RAM Club held its end-of-term social at the Holborn Restaurant on July 21, 1919, and this restaurant and the Central Hall were to feature in Jenkins's private life.

In March or April 1919 Jenkins organized a group of his black friends into a social club which they called The Coterie of Friends. A constitution was printed, stating that the club was "to further social intercourse amongst young men of colour, resident or temporarily resident in Great Britain; to provide its members with a library containing books and papers relating to people of colour." The secretary was the pharmacy student Harold Piper, and the treasurer the law student Randall Lockhart. The British Guiana law student Lionel Mitchell and law student Adderley had both been at the APU meeting, and were members of the Coterie, according to a list of ten names dated December 1919. Others included medical student Harry Leekam, the forty-two-year-old Gold Coast merchant E. A. Manyo Plange, and the Jamaica-born California gold mine owner Thaddeus E. Walker. Alphonso Luke from Trinidad was a member, but his occupation has been untraced, and nothing is known of R. H. Price.

The group would have subscribed to the London weekly *West Africa*, the editor of which, Albert Cartwright, had been at the APU dinner. Cartwright reported the speeches in his magazine from the beginning of January, receiving the thanks of Barbour-James in a letter published on March 29, 1919. They would have purchased copies of John Eldred Taylor's *The African Telegraph,* which detailed the growing racial antagonisms including, in April 1919, a "great fight at Winchester camp between American whites and African troops." From America they would obtain *The Crisis,* which was devoting more of its space to detailing lynching incidents in the United States and the race conflicts as black peasants from the South moved North to break away from peonage and take jobs in America's growing industries. The editor of the NAACP's *The Crisis* was Du Bois, who had traveled to France in early 1919 to press the black cause at the peace negotiations. He joined forces with Archer and Taylor, but these blacks comprised one of many such pressure groups; one comment on these days was "Paris was a happy hunting ground for delegations of small disgruntled and discontented groups."[11]

Leekam, Jeffers, Jenkins, Lockhart, Piper, and the others continued to aid black troops in London, entertaining them at the Iles's home. Other well wishers helped the thousands of foreign guests in Britain. The huge civilian armies were anxious to return to normal life and were impatient of the politicians who still talked in Paris. Bitter fighting continued in Ireland, in towns in Germany and eastern Europe, and the British and French military action against the new Soviet Union dragged on. Vast numbers of men in labor battalions were clearing the millions of tons of rubble, shells, barbed wire, poison gas shells, and debris of the trench warfare. Politicians, who had given up much of their factional views to help in the war, returned to the debate, anxious to make up for the lost years. In Britain the police went on strike. Soldiers and sailors returned home, to find that their old jobs had been taken up by others. The winter of 1918–1919 saw millions die from influenza.

In the United States and in Britain the black community was the victim of violence. Martial law was imposed in Charleston in May after white sailors killed one black.[12] Race riots broke out in the coaling port of Cardiff in south Wales in June; the immediate postwar boom there had been followed by a slump, which, combined with exservicemen returning to find their jobs and women taken by blacks, led to conflict.[13] The *Times* reported on June 12 "Race Riots At Cardiff—White Man Killed," and "Negroes beaten with frying pans." Two days later it reported "Irishman and Negro Shot" and that the police in the port of Liverpool took into custody over fifty people on charges connected with race riots in that city. Violence was not only directed against blacks. Canadian troops in the English town of Epsom raided a police station and killed the sergeant.[14]

The visitors to the peace negotiations arrived from Africa, including, in May, Charles D. B. King, the President-elect of Liberia. King joined Thomas McCants Stewart, the Charleston-born lawyer who had emigrated to Liberia before the war because of U.S. race bigotry, and who had been in London throughout the war years.[15] King was to journey to the United States to beg a loan from the federal government. America had its own troubles; race riots had broken out in many U.S. cities, including the nation's capital in July, and Chicago where riots raged from July 27 for three days before the mayor called in the militia. Fifteen whites and twenty-three blacks died in Chicago and over five hundred were injured. Cartwright's *West Africa* wrote about the "disgraceful outbreak in Chicago," explaining that "the war brought several hundred thousand of the darker race into Chicago as hand workers, and the fear, unfounded as we believe, that these would work at under union rates largely accounts for the outbreak."[16]

While blacks in uniform were killed, and whites in uniform took a leading part in disturbances in American race riots, the authorities in Britain had sent in military vehicles to stop the street fighting in Cardiff.[17] The economic nature of the British riots is indicated by an article in *West Africa* in mid-August 1919 telling of the deliberate attack by the Liverpool mob on a liquor store and bottling company, which was held by drunken looters for fourteen hours, in which over £10,000 ($50,000) of damage was caused. A million bottles of beer and stout were in the hands of the mob. Finally, children of the streets sold stolen bottles to the general public.

On July 18, 1919, three days before the RAM Club gathering, the black friends of Jenkins, including Piper and Plange, met at the Holborn Restaurant in London, where the APU and another black-interest group, the Society of People of African Origin, were supposed to merge. It is likely that Jenkins had contributed toward the £1,600 ($8,000) collected by the group, intended to build hostels for blacks in London, Liverpool, and Cardiff.[18] In the same month President-elect C. D. B. King of Liberia met King George V, the first official meeting between the British monarch and the head of the Republic of Liberia since Joseph Jenkins Roberts had met Queen Victoria.

Edmund Jenkins had been away from the United States for five years, and his studies at the Royal Academy of Music were due to continue, for he was awarded the wind instrument Ross Scholarship for the two years beginning September 1919. He and his friends in the Coterie were very busy in the summer of 1919, contacting the various visiting black politicians and race leaders who passed through London and arranging gatherings of blacks from west Africa, south Africa, the Caribbean, and the United States. The 1915 proposals of Gus Haston for a "big colored orchestra" had finally been concluded and Will Marion Cook's orchestra had arrived in London.

CHAPTER **10**

JAZZ COMES TO EUROPE

Will Marion Cook's orchestra arrived in Liverpool in early July 1919, but these musicians were not the first visiting American entertainers to play to war-weary Britons. The changes in musical taste that had taken place in America had been delayed in Europe because of the fighting from mid-1914, and it was with great enthusiasm that Europeans took up public dancing and jazz. *Musical Progress*, a London monthly, said in its June 1, 1919, issue:

> What with jazz bands and banjo bands, which bid fair to eclipse one another in popularity, the genuine orchestra seems to be "resting". Whatever may be said regarding this craze, it seems, at any rate, to be a welcome relief after the last four or five years' strain, and even the hardest critics cannot find great fault with the rage, only that it is nerve-racking to sensitive folk.

The Original Dixieland Jazz Band had been the rage of New York in 1916 and had sold thousands of copies of its 1917 recordings across America. The band arrived in England to take part in a stage review at London's Hippodrome, but the star there, George Robey, took exception to them. From April 1919 they, therefore, toured the variety circuits of Britain and recorded. Their appearances and records spread the new jazz music across Britain and encouraged local imitations. The fast and frantic playing involved skilled musical knowledge, an ability to improvise on a simple melody, and stamina, for the jazz groups were only four or five musicians (the ODJB was a quintet). Successful groups were well paid—one quartet was paid £40 ($200) a night in early 1919.[1] The music was not easy to play, as one experienced musician recalled: "Any good musician who had a feeling and a flair for playing the new syncopated dance music found himself in a lucrative line of business. Actually such musicians were in short supply."[2]

Some British musicians could play the new music, and it was an English ragtime pianist, Billy Jones, who replaced the ODJB's J. Russel Robinson in the late summer of 1919. The other four members of the ODJB were Tony Sbarbaro (drums), Nick La Rocca (cornet), Emile Christian (trombone), and Larry Shields (clarinet). The ODJB played at the Savoy Hotel peace treaty celebrations of June 28, 1919.[3] By the following week Shields was not the only clarinetist from New Orleans in London, for Cook had brought Sidney Bechet, a New Orleans musician who had been in Chicago when Cook was arranging his London trip.

Cook's orchestra, The Southern Syncopated Orchestra, played at London's Philharmonic Hall, just around the corner from the Queen's Hall, from July 4, 1919. Finances may have come from Joe Jordan.[4] Their show was a mixture of singing and orchestrated playing, with an informal atmosphere in the minstrel show tradition. The show was very popular, and the Southern Syncopated Orchestra (SSO) played extra matinees at the Prince of Wales Theater later in the year.[5] The thirty-six to fifty musicians with Cook included two veterans of the Jenkins Orphanage musicians, Ed and Jacob Patrick.[6] They or Cook would have told Edmund Jenkins of James Reese Europe's murder in Boston that May, when he fell victim to ex-Orphanage Herbert Wright, who lost his temper.[7] William Arthur Briggs, another Charleston musician in the SSO, was a West Indian (or Canadian black) who had studied with Eugene Mikell.[8] The drummer was Buddy Gilmore, who had played with James Europe's band, and another cornet player was E. E. Thompson, who had been assistant bandleader of the 15th New York Infantry Band, which had become the 369 Infantry Band under Europe and Mikell in France.[9] Randall Lockhart recalled the SSO sixty years later: "They took London by storm and privately they were a hectic crowd, so that a good time was had by all."[10]

The socialist George Lansbury was editing a London newspaper *The Daily Herald* in 1919, and he published details of an interview with Cook in the paper on Friday, August 1, 1919, in which Cook referred to the Chicago riots of that week, saying "Instead of being President of all the people in the United States of America President Wilson has tried absolutely to close the door of hope to the negro." Lansbury saw the SSO, commenting on August 2, on "their rousing ragtime and ensemble singing." On the Sunday he employed them at the People's Palace in east London (later Queen Mary's College) and was struck by Bechet's musicianship. *The Daily Herald* of August 4 mentions "Mr. Sydney [*sic*] Bechet did some strange things with the clarionet, aptly called 'Characteristic Blues.' "

At the end of that week the Coterie of Friends organized a gathering "in honour of an international group of representatives of the Colonial race now visiting London, the delegates including men from Sierra Leone, the Gold Coast, and Liberia."[11] The host and hostess were Judge Thomas McCants Stewart and his wife, and Jenkins, described in the report in *West Africa* as "student sub-professor in the Royal Academy of Music" was "responsible for the excellent concert." Gathered in the Albert Rooms, off central London's Tottenham Court Road, on that Friday night, August 8, 1919, were Jenkins, the McCants Stewarts, Lockhart, Piper, and Mitchell. Their guests included the South African Native National Congress (SANNC) delegation which was headed by Sol Plaatje. His four colleagues were Henry Reed Ngcayiya, an official of the Ethiopian Church of South Africa, whose son was a schoolteacher in America[12]; R. V. Selope-Thema, who was the secretary of the delegation[13]; L. T. Mvabaza, the managing director of *Abantu Batho*, the official organ of the SANNC founded in 1912; and Josiah Gumede, later a radical figure in south Africa.[14] They had been joined in England by another black south African, M. Xaba, a theology student who was returning from studies in the United States.[15]

From British Guiana were A. B. Brown, E. G. Woolford, the Rev. E. Robertson, and J. McFarlene Cory. The Gold Coast visitor was Manyo Plange, and Sierra Leone was represented by William and F. T. Dove. Frans Thomas Dove was a brilliant lawyer, and his son, Frank S. Dove, had been at Oxford University when he had enlisted in the British army, joining the elite Tank Corps, fighting bravely at the battle of Cambrai (the first breach of the German lines in over three years) to be awarded the coveted Military Medal.[16] His uncle Frederick William Dove was a Freetown municipal councilor and businessman.[17] Frank Dove's sister Evelyn Dove was also at this gathering, and she was a close friend of the Coterie, eventually marrying Luke.[18]

West Africa's report of August 16 spells Plaatje's name as "Plaatge" (it is pronounced Plaai-kie), and John Richard Archer is listed as "G. R. Archer," exmayor of Battersea. John Eldred Taylor was also present. So were members of Will Marion Cook's orchestra. The violinist Angelita Riveira played Jenkins's *Reverie Phantasy* with Jenkins (piano). Ada Parker then played the piano, Jenkins the clarinet, and Riveira the violin in the *Allegro Sostenuto* by Eaton Faning. Jenkins played Weber's Clarinet Concerto in F, and Coleridge-Taylor's *Canoe Song* was sung by Evelyn Dove. She then sang Jenkins's lullaby *Baby Mine*, written by Jenkins according to *West Africa* but actually another Plowright-Jenkins collaboration.[19] Coleridge-Taylor's *A Lament* was also presented.

> At the end of the musical programme the audience kept up such an enthusiastic demonstration that Mr. Jenkins felt compelled to come forward and acknowledge it. Then, noting the presence of Mr. Marion Cook, the leader of the Southern Syncopated Orchestra, someone called out "Cook! Cook!" and Mr. Cook came forward and bowed his appreciation.[20]

Another London weekly, *The African World,* reported Harold Piper's speech on August 23, 1919:

> He stated that the object of the club was that of bringing together the coloured people in London, primarily in order that they may get to know one another much better than heretofore, for, in this great busy city, there was very little social friendliness. Another ambition of the club was the unification of the African and the Afro-American peoples into one consolidated whole. He said that the day was now at hand when the coloured people the world over should, with one united front, stand shoulder to shoulder in order that they may obtain that place in the sun which is theirs by right but which they will fail to obtain if they keep apart.

Piper and Jenkins had invited to the gathering many important people, including the African explorer, administrator, linguist, and author Sir Harry Johnston, whose ill health prevented him from attending, and Charles D. B. King of Liberia, who had left for the United States a few days earlier.[21] His apologies were expressed by Stewart, who said that King "regretted keenly that he was compelled to miss the honour of being present there that night. The significance of that assembly could not be over-estimated." Stewart's speech expressed the mood of the gathering, for he added "Thoughtful men were beginning to feel and to say that there must be more brotherhood, unlimited by race or colour, if the world was to avert the greatest calamity it had ever experienced, namely a war of races. The world could not get into a state of rest while part of it knew no colour line in the enjoyment of public and civil rights, and another part erected a colour bar." Stewart remarked that "Britain to-day was in danger of coming under the rule of the spirit of South Africa, whose people regarded dark-skinned men as their inferiors."

Sol Plaatje spoke for the black south Africans, who were seeking a restoration of British justice in South African affairs, which had been internally self-governing since 1910. Black south Africans wanted "educational facilities and the right to become skilled artisans, and above all, the right to vote, even if based upon some qualification as education or a poll tax or ownership of property."[23] Plaatje was to visit the United States in his search for justice in southern Africa. Plaatje's biographer Brian Willan has located evidence that Plaatje had met the Jenkins band at the White City in 1914, and it is now known that he lived a few hundred yards from the Barbour-James family in Acton, west London, in 1916. He was a translator, journalist, and poet with a considerable musical ear. He had been influenced by Orpheus McAdoo, the North Carolina minstrel,[24] and seems to have had knowledge of the Colwyn Bay Institute, because his brother-in-law had suggested in 1903 that young Jabavu went there.[25]

William Dove spoke for the west Africans, saying that they wanted more participation in government, fewer restrictions that excluded natives from the civil service, and an enlargement of commercial opportunities, a criticism of the large, often Liverpool-based, British companies in control of much of west African trade.

Brown spoke, and so did George Lattimore, the black New Yorker who managed the SSO. "The rest of the evening was spent in social converse and dancing."[26] The gossip columnist of *West Africa* reported that "Music for the dancing, which was kept up till 5 A.M., was provided by Mr. Cook, the genius of the Southern Syncopated Orchestra (which is attracting London to the Philharmonic Hall each day) and some of his colleagues."[27]

Over sixty years later Briggs recalled the "friendly gathering with members of the group" and named the others as Johnny Rayne, Carrol Morgan, Lottie Gee, Joe Jones, and Mrs. King Reavis.[28] Hattie King Reavis was in contact with Jenkins some time in London on a matter not detailed in her note dated just "Wednesday 8th" on SSO London paper.

Despite the late night, Briggs, with Bechet, William Forrester (trombone), and drummer Robert Young played on Saturday, August 9 at a garden party at Buckingham Palace, held to celebrate the June 28 peace treaty, and given for the Palace police, servants, and their families.[29] King George V attended, and over one thousand staff were in the palace grounds[30] watching Cook's SSO and Bechet, Briggs, and the others in a "Nigger Jazz Band."[31] Bechet's autobiography suggests that this was a Royal Command Performance, but it was a garden party. The cast of *In Dahomey* had also played at the Palace in June, 1903, an event also recollected as important in the history of black endeavors. The acceptance of American blacks by the British monarchy indicated that white American attitudes were not always the attitude of whites, and it is well established that black entertainers returning to the United States encouraged their friends to question American racism.

While in London Bechet and Briggs purchased a soprano saxophone that was to make a unique contribution to black recordings in New York from 1924. Young was to work with Edmund Jenkins in Baltimore in early 1924.

"M. B." of *West Africa* interviewed Will Marion Cook, and nearly the whole of page 739 of the issue for August 30, 1919, is devoted to this interview, which included Cook's comments: "The American coloured man . . . still regards Africa as his home. By accident of birth, he may be a citizen of another country, but inborn there is always the love of Africa in every coloured man's heart." Cook was not the only American in London interested in going "back to

Africa." William L. Patterson, a black lawyer, had arrived in London with the news of McCants Stewart's son's suicide. He discussed emigration to Liberia with Stewart, whose opinion on American black opportunities had changed from his 1885 reports of how safe he felt in Columbia, South Carolina. But Liberia didn't need lawyers and musicians from America: it needed artisans, people with knowledge of industry, commerce, and engineering.[32] Liberia was insolvent, partly because of its ill-judged declaration of war on Germany. Edmund Jenkins would have discussed emigration with his roommate Piper and with his various black friends. His opportunity for success was music—both classical, from his training with Corder, and popular dance/jazz, from his background in the orphanage brass bands and his feeling for the rhythms, interpretation, and structure of American popular music. Together these talents gave him great advantages over Europeans. As a Ross Scholar at the academy Edmund Jenkins was studying with Augarde again, as well as taking harmony with Corder, and piano from Vivian Langrish, who had returned from military service with the air force.

At about the time he was to begin his sixth year at the Royal Academy, Edmund Jenkins was offered the leadership of Will Marion Cook's Southern Syncopated Orchestra; the group had split over money, and Cook had returned to the United States, leaving George Lattimore anxious to obtain a musical director of Cook's talents. The Haitian-born Bertin Salnave, who was two years older than Jenkins, and studying in France when Lattimore employed him, was in London by September 1919. Salnave recalled, "When Will Marion Cook left us, Lattimore sought the help of the respected coloured musician Edmund Jenkins, son of the well-known director of the Jenkins Orphan Asylum in Charleston."[33] Salnave recalled that "Both Edmund Jenkins and another musician, whose name escapes me, declined the post, so Lattimore committed the direction of the orchestra to trumpeter E. E. Thompson." Jenkins did not ignore his fellow black Americans in the SSO, for he was to utilize four of them at a concert in London in December, in which he and his colleagues of the Coterie of Friends presented a concert of Coleridge-Taylor's works to an audience that included the composer's widow and daughter, and Sir Charles Villiers Stanford, his tutor.

CHAPTER 11

ONE OF THE RISING
HOPES OF HIS RACE

The Coterie of Friends held a concert in London on November 2, 1919, which may have been the presentation of Gounod's *Redemption* mentioned in an American magazine, *Opportunity*, in late 1925. The *Redemption* would have been to commemorate the first anniversary of the armistice, a solemn occasion in Britain, with all traffic halting in memory of the dead. It was also a time of celebration, and Plaatje and other south Africans joined the Southern Syncopated Orchestra at the Philharmonic Hall and afterwards, at a dance at the Albert Hall in the evening of November 11, 1919.[1] Edmund Jenkins's Sierra Leone friend John Eldred Taylor, who has been described as "a company promoter, floating a string of interconnected and dubious companies with slender assets and extravagant aspirations,"[2] was in financial and legal trouble in November; his *African Telegraph* had published, in December 1918, an article "Flogging of Women Naked in Nigeria," which led to a libel case heard that month. Lansbury reported the case in *The Daily Herald* and also reported the "Edinburgh Castle" incident when the SANNC delegation of black Africans, without Plaatje, who was on his way to America, was removed from the passenger liner of that name at the request of the white South African troops on board, whose racist views could not tolerate these black men as fellow passengers.[3] Before the delegation had left England they had been able to see Prime Minister David Lloyd George at the House of Commons on November 21. With the SANNC group at Westminster were Taylor, Hughes, Barbour-James, and the Nigerian journalist Thomas Horatio Jackson.[4] Sol Plaatje was in New York when the Coterie produced their Coleridge-Taylor concert in London's Wigmore Hall on the afternoon of Sunday, December 7, 1919. The twenty names of distinguished guests at the concert listed in *West Africa* on December 13, 1919, included Taylor, and Jenkins's friends Audrey Jeffers, Cecilia Amado Taylor, Miss Sapara (probably the daughter of the Sierra Leone Dr. Oguntola Sapara who worked in Lagos), and Robert Broadhurst; Barbour-James's good friend A. S. Cann, a merchant from the Gold Coast with offices in London; and Anthony and Jeanette Tuck, the Americans who were with Gus Haston in The Versatile Three, which had been in London for months. Also listed is S. W. Duncan from Nigeria.

The concert had been announced in *West Africa*, which said that it was a tribute to the greatest musical composer of the African race, and added "Mr. Edmund T. Jenkins, who will be the first coloured conductor, other than Coleridge-Taylor himself, to render his work before a British audience. Miss Coleridge-Taylor, the late composer's daughter, will contribute a musical monologue, set to music by her father."[5] Jenkins paid fourteen guineas to the Wigmore Hall authorities on November 25, 1919, and Piper went to W. H. Smith's Railway Advertising Department at 186 Strand in central London on November 28, and paid one pound for a week's advertising of twenty-five posters on the book and newspaper stalls operated by Smiths on the London railway system.

On November 29 *West Africa* gave some publicity to the concert, which was "almost exclusively dedicated to the works of Coleridge-Taylor." The other item to be presented was "a 'Folk Rhapsody,' by that clever young composer, Mr. E. T. Jenkins, Ross Scholar, R.A.M., under whose direction the concert is being held. Mr. H. R. Piper, 51 Westbere Road, West Hampstead, N.W. 2., will supply tickets, 3s 6d to 12s., and further information." Harold Piper's home was between Sumatra Road and Archer Plowright's home in Pine Road, Cricklewood, not far from the Iles.

The twelve-page souvenir program includes the list of the members of the Coterie of Friends, including the unknown Price. It has a picture of a serious-looking Edmund Jenkins (also found in *West*

Africa December 13, 1919) and a biographical note on Coleridge-Taylor by Randall Lockhart. Coleridge-Taylor's widow, daughter, and tutor (Sir Charles Stanford) were at the Wigmore Hall that afternoon. The concert was:

> *Symphonic Variations – On an African Air*
> Song – *Hiawatha's Vision* (soloist Mrs. W. A. Michael)
> *Scenes From an Imaginary Ballet*
> Concerto in G minor (violin solo: Winifred Small)
> Monologue – *The Clown and Columbine* (Gwendolen
>   Coleridge-Taylor) with violin, cello, and piano
> Folk Rhapsody written by Edmund Jenkins
> Songs – *Sons of the Sea*, and *Beat, Beat Drums* (soloist
>   Mrs. Michael)
> March – *Ethiopia Saluting the Colours*

The program notes were written by Wendell Bruce James, the Caribbean black organist and pianist who eventually joined the SSO.[6] James wrote:

> Mr. Jenkins, though as yet little known to the musical world at large, has obtained an enviable reputation among those who do know him, as one of the rising hopes of his race in the sphere of Art Music. An American by birth, he has had a brilliant career at the Royal Academy of Music in London. The work to be played today under his baton may justly be regarded as the first-fruits of his undoubtedly high talent.

The composition, wrote James, was:

> entirely rhapsodic. After a short introduction, based upon an original theme, we hear from the Solo Horn a characteristic Negro melody. This at once begins a dialogue with the Solo Violin, the latter playing the well-known Negro folk song or spiritual "Swing low, Sweet chariot." With tempo moderato we arrive at another well-known air, "Nobody knows de trouble I see, Lord." These three themes from the melodic back-bone of the whole work, and we have them alone, or in combination, during the progress of the whole piece, up to the

brilliant climax with which it terminates. This composition is, as a Folk Rhapsody should be, full of rhythmic and characteristically racial vitality.

The first theme of Jenkins's work was probably a Charleston black fisherman's song, which would have been unknown to James. It may have been known to the Charleston-educated Arthur Briggs, who sat in the trumpet section with Frank James and Miss K. Lucas.

Other black musicians from the SSO in the fifty-four piece orchestra under Jenkins's direction were Bertin Salnave, the principal flute, who later recalled "It was he (Jenkins) who revealed the worth of Coleridge-Taylor's compositions"[7]; Santos Rivera, a Puerto Rican who was one of the three double-bass players; and Frank Withers, one of the three trombonists. Briggs remembered the concert sixty years later telling German researcher Rainer Lotz, "I can never forget this wonderful memory, although I was scared to death."[8]

The fifty British musicians included Winifred Small, Jean Pougnet, John Barbirolli, and members of three very musical families, the James, Borsdorf, and Brain clans. Jenkins was to study the oboe and the bassoon with E. Fred James, whose brother, Frank James, was the principal trumpet that afternoon. (The third brother was bassoonist with the Queen's Hall Orchestra). Principal horn Adolph Borsdorf played the Charleston theme in the *Rhapsody*; he was principal horn at Covent Garden and in other orchestras as well. His son, who changed his surname to Bradley, was second horn that afternoon. Next to Francis Bradley was Miss Lucas, a student, and fourth horn was A. E. Brain, whose father Alfred and brother Aubrey were horn players, too. His nephew Dennis Brain was to win the 1938 Ross Scholarship. Jenkins had the finest horn players in Britain for his concert.

Alfred Adderley and Lionel Mitchell completed their law studies in late 1919, and most of the other members of the Coterie were still studying with little opportunity of extracurricular activities providing any income. Manyo Plange's cocoa trading business was substantial, but since he was often out of London it seems reasonable to assume that it was Edmund Jenkins who provided the cash for the Wigmore Hall concert.[9] He may have worked during vacations with Haston, Tuck, and Mills of the Versatile Three, which also worked as a quartet. He may have obtained funds from arranging music, for Louisville, Kentucky, black W. H. Dorsey had arranged music for the Versatile Three in mid-1918[10] and there are suggestions that Jenkins played with Tuck and Haston. The Versatile Three had a fine reputation in British entertainment, and were appearing at Hammersmith in the first week of September, 1919, with the white black-face entertainer G. H. Elliott. Jenkins's fees for teaching Miss Harrison were only three and a half guineas (£3.68p, or $17) for the whole year, and he had enough money to be able to lend his good friend Harold Piper one hundred pounds by mid-December 1919.

Harold Piper had completed his pharmacy studies and was preparing to leave London to travel to Trinidad one week after the Wigmore Hall concert. The friends gathered at the home of Edmund Jenkins, some rooms or an apartment at 36 Bloomsbury Street in the area of small hotels, guest houses, and inexpensive lodgings near the British Museum. Piper had become a Member of the Pharmaceutical Society of London, had joined the ancient Company of Spectaclemakers, and had become a Freeman of the City of London.[11] A celebration dinner was held at 36 Bloomsbury Street on Friday, December 12, starting at seven. Jenkins kept the typed souvenir menu, which was signed by Piper, the two Leekam brothers, and their English girl friends "Mabs" Trollope and "Mimi" Durkin, Randall Lockhart, Henry Gordon Andrews, Clifford Richardson, J. Rby. Macdougall, Eugene Escallier, and Madeleine Calcull. Lockhart recalled the Coterie of Friends sixty years later: "Most of them were or are West Indians and in those days we were just students and in a sense nonentities."[12] Amy "Mimi" Durkin, who married "Harry" Leekam, recalled Edmund Jenkins in a letter dated July 1980: "Yes I do remember 'Teddy'—as we called him—very well, a wonderful musician and pianist. He often visited us in Golders Green . . . he amused my parents and myself by playing the piano at home . . . his favourite opera was 'Tosca.' "[13] On several occasions Jenkins went to Miss Durkin's home, which was a fifteen-minute bus ride from Sumatra Road, and took snapshots of the family. "He visited us many times and my parents were very fond of him and his music."

Harold Piper wrote a letter to "my dear Jenks" from the Royal

Pier Hotel in Southampton on December 13, while he waited for the boat to the Caribbean. The friends had seen Piper off at the London rail terminus that morning. The letter asks Jenkins to "thank them all for their many kind statements of this morning and in my turn once more wish them a successful time and pray that things may be so altered that Boscher will see them less frequently and that ozone lunches will soon end," a reference, no doubt, to a pawnbroker and to the usual student diet when money from home is overdue. Piper hoped, "May they all keep up the fight and emerge each and every one a man beloved by his people and respected by the whites." Referring to Jenkins, Lockhart, and Leekam as his "dearest friends," Piper wrote "To you three especially do I look for maintaining the great work that we *must* have done."

Attached to his letter was a statement of his indebtedness, totaling £100 ($485). It was made up of "previous loans £10, Luke £5" and "recently £1, £5, £5" and "bal. on suit £8–10s," which suggests that Piper had purchased a new and rather expensive suit for his return home.[14] The remaining money was paid to Piper by checks.

Piper was on board the *Tunisian*, waiting for it to sail, on December 14, 1919, when he found time to write to his London friends whom he was unlikely to see again. "I had a little adventure this morning when, on taking up the berth corresponding with the particulars on my ticket, I found that the other occupants were all women. One of them tried to be nasty and said something sotto voce about 'black man.' After a little while, however, I had them at ease and they took the matter as I did—that is, as a huge joke." His correct cabin companions were whites—"they appear to be fairly decent chaps and I don't believe there will be any unpleasantness." Also traveling to the Caribbean were a few exsoldiers being repatriated by the army, and a dozen Trinidad-bound passengers who, with Piper, would change ships. Piper's note to "my dear Jenkins" ends with the postscript "Keep 'The Coterie of Friends' alive."

Benjamin Brawley wrote to Jenkins on December 13, 1919, saying

> When you wrote you were uncertain about work or returning to this country. Once more I hope that you are remaining close to all the ideals we have cherished. Over here I have said that you were the most promising musician we had in all the

world. And now what do you think? If you are still in England as I hope you are, it is very likely that within a few weeks we may see each other. Mrs. Brawley and I are expecting to arrive in Liverpool about the end of January. What for? Well, I have on hand about the biggest thing that has ever happened to me. Three responsible agencies in or near New York are sending me as their joint representative and as a teacher in Liberia College, Monrovia, Liberia. The contract is for one term only, for the school year is from March until November; but I can do more with it than that if I wish. The main thing, however, is that whilst ostensibly I shall be a teacher my mission will have much wider scope than the work of a mere teacher. All *that* I could better explain in person than write to you.

It does not appear that the Brawleys were able to travel to Liberia in 1920, but they were able to meet Jenkins, who went back to the United States in August 1920 during the vacation from the Royal Academy of Music. Edmund Jenkins was able to pay for the ten-thousand-mile round trip from his earnings in the entertainment world of Britain, where his abilities and understanding of the so-called new music made him one of the more successful band leaders.

CHAPTER **12**

THE LORD MAYOR
SHOOK HIS HAND

In November 1919 the Original Dixieland Jazz Band had settled into a regular position as one of the two dance bands at the new Palais de Danse in west London's Hammersmith, and the new music was very popular in Britain. There is confusion in the contemporary press over the meaning of the word *jazz*, which appears to have been a drum kit, according to advertisements in the trade paper *Musical Progress* as early as May 1919. The same magazine, in November 1919, commented "The shortage of dancing halls is as acute as the shortage of theatres, and all kinds of halls are being converted, from church meeting rooms to old skating rinks."

The black Americans in Lattimore's Southern Syncopated Orchestra saw opportunities in the dance and jazz-mad Britain and left to form small groups with local white musicians. These groups toured throughout the country, and it became fashionable to have a black member of a modern dance band, indicating that the music was "genuine." Africans and West Indians in Britain took the opportunity to cash in on their popular appeal and their color advantage, and soon the SSO had Bruce James, Frank Lacton (who had been organist at the cathedral in Freetown, Sierra Leone), and Gold Coast student William Ofori from Coleridge-Taylor's father's old school in Taunton, Somerset.

Edmund Jenkins was unable to tour due to his studies in London, but he established a dance band in the chamber music hall in the roof of the Queen's Hall in Langham Place. Like the main hall, the small hall had a flat floor, making it suitable for dancing, and it was a few steps above the pavement, an ideal venue for the new music. Shaw described the hall in 1894 as "the most comfortable of our small concert-rooms, though, as I am unfortunately a bad sailor, its cigar shape and the windows in the ceiling suggest a steamer saloon so strongly that I have hardly yet got over the qualmishness which attacked me when I first entered it."[1]

In 1919 Mr. and Mrs. Walter Cave carried out some alterations[2] to the small hall, and Jenkins joined with pianist Claude Ivy to entertain the London crowd. Harry Leekam recalled something of these days in an interview in Trinidad in 1980 "Jenkins played at Madame Henry's dancehall on Regent St. He earned a very good salary there—fifty pounds a week. He was very versatile and could do 'everything connected with the stage.' He was extremely popular at Madame Henry's."[3]

In the fall of 1919 Claude Ivy, who demonstrated piano music during the day, was joined at his music publishing company by Jack Hylton, who had been a music hall entertainer who had been serving in the army during the war. Hylton wrote, years later, "Claude then was undoubtedly a very big shot, having become associated with the then very famous Queen's Hall Roof dancing resort in a most curious band which operated there."[4] Hylton was employed by Ivy and Jenkins as relief or interval pianist. Ivy, described by Hylton as "that technical master of the piano,"[5] had a drinking problem,[6] and Hylton became the regular pianist. Hylton, Britain's most popular band leader between the wars, described the band as "a real ragtime affair, busking choruses in woeful harmony to a background of kitchen furniture noises manipulated by young Harry Robbins . . . there were two saxophonists and a long-neck G-banjo player. Virtually the only schooled musician in the outfit was a coloured clarinettist by the name of Jenkins, who was actually a professor on his instrument at the Royal Academy and could read. Another member of the band who could read was Johnny Rosen, on violin."[7]

Hylton's recollections were different than those of Harry Leekam, who had left Britain in the early 1930s, and recalled events in 1980. Jenkins "was in charge of the orchestra there until an Englishman named Jack Hylton came on the scene. Hylton was jealous of Jenkins and wanted to control everything. He caused some problems which caused Jenkins to relinquish the position in disgust. Jenkins had been one of two black musicians in the band."[8]

In documents found in Charleston in 1979 were several photographic negatives, including shots of people outside the Queen's Hall, and one of Bert Bassett, the banjo player in this band. The manager of the roof night club was Herbert Henry (by fashionable sophistication it became "Henri"), who was in contact with the Paris music supply firm of Albert Behar by early 1920. Their reply dated February 28, 1920, was also found in Charleston in 1979. As it concerns the prices of clarinets, it indicates that Herbert Henry and Edmund Jenkins were close friends by late 1919, which is best explained by his position as leader or joint leader of a popular and profitable dance band at the Queen's Hall Roof. The Queen's Hall Roof was to be a major influence on Edmund Jenkins and, through his 1921 recordings, on British musicians. It gave Edmund Jenkins a considerable income, which enabled him to dress smartly and to obtain a camera that was capable of taking indoor pictures. His photographic subjects included Ferdie Leekam, Winifred Small, Jean Pougnet in knee pants outside the academy, Frederick Corder, and his tennis-playing white friends.

He was also able to lend his friends money. Clifford A. Richardson, who had been one of the guests at Piper's farewell dinner, wrote to him from 94 Paisley Road in the southern coastal resort town of Bournemouth, on February 4, 1920, saying, "I hope to be able to settle up with you as soon as I get to London. There is one other person besides myself who feels deeply indebted to you but of that I shall speak when I see you." A clue as to the person's identity may be found in the fact that living at 66 Paisley Road at this time was the eighty-three-year-old Thomas Lewis Johnson, evangelist, exslave, associate of Spurgeon, Hodder, Williams, and the Congo Institute. Johnson's first wife, with her sister and the latter's husband, C. H. Richardson, had traveled with Johnson to Africa many years before. It seems likely that Jenkins's friend was related to the black missionary Richardson and that Jenkins had lent the elderly Rev. Johnson some money. This possible linking of Britain's black community over a period of fifty years is yet to be proven; however, Clifford A. Richardson's letter referred to many of Jenkins's friends: "Have you any news of Piper? He is in Trinidad, by now, I'm sure. Jenkins, Old Boy, you are a Good Samaritan." He mentions Andrews, the Trinidad businessman who had been at Piper's farewell dinner, and Wendell Phillips, about whom nothing has been traced, and "Mrs. Iles and family have asked me to remember them to you. They are all as hail and hearty as ever. Rita especially wants to be remembered."

Randall Lockhart recalled his days with Edmund Jenkins before his return to the Caribbean in late 1922. "Jenkins was acquainted with most if not all the outstanding American Negro Musicians of those days. Roland Hayes, Harry T. Burleigh, Will Marion Cook. The last named came to London with his Southern Syncopated Orchestra. He and his band rendered music of more popular appeal than did Hayes or Burleigh."[9]

In May 1920 Hayes arrived in London.[10] He was traveling with his pianist Lawrence Brown, and they gave performances in London, including at the Wigmore Hall. Lawrence Brown became a friend of Jenkins and the Leekams. The group of students broke up as they qualified and returned to their homes to start a new chapter. Lionel Mitchell and Alfred Adderley completed their law studies in late 1919 and, like Harold Piper, went to the Caribbean. Felix Hercules went to the United States.[11] The lives of others in the group had changed in other ways as well: John Eldred Taylor's *African Telegraph* had been bankrupt and his only daughter had died in the influenza epidemic.[12] His brother Henry died in London.[13] Adderley had told the APU gathering of December 1918 that he had been told of Africa by Mr. J. C. Smith. James Carmichael Smith, an associate of Dusé Mohammed Ali, was also from the Bahamas, and had been the Postmaster General of Sierra Leone from 1900 until late 1911. Smith had associated with Sir Samuel Lewis, the black knight who was involved with Colwyn Bay's Institute, and may have been introduced to Adderley by Barbour-James, who, like Smith, worked in the London civil service from 1917 although retired. Smith died in London in October 1919 less than two weeks after Henry Taylor.[14]

John Barbour-James had been very ill in mid-1919, and was unable to attend the funeral of his youngest daughter Millicent on June 18, 1919. "Tony" Tuck and Gus Haston were friends of Jenkins and Lockhart, and the group became more American as the SSO members made friends with the Caribbean and African blacks of London. Evelyn Dove eventually worked with the SSO. Her brother Frank was back at Oxford, reading law. The Acham-Chens were in London where Percy was studying law. Alexander Hutton-Mills had been studying at Keble College, Oxford; Thomas Hutton-Mills was at Adderley's old Cambridge college, Saint Catharine's; and their sister Violet, who had been studying in Brighton, fifty miles south of London, since 1912, was studying music at a London music college.[15] The exploitation of the cocoa of the Gold Coast and the edible oils of Nigeria had enabled many west Africans to send their children to Britain, and Cartwright's *West Africa* had become "the intelligent African's guide to current affairs."[16] Thomas Jackson, the Nigerian publisher of the *Lagos Weekly Record*, attempted to provide a newspaper to blacks in Britain, but his *The African Sentinel* made few sales after its first appearance in January 1920, and Jackson returned to Africa. During his months in England Jackson had become a member of the Essex County Cricket Club,[17] and this very British summer sport, which was followed with great enthusiasm in the British West Indies, attracted Harry Leekam from his medical studies.[18] His younger brother "paid more attention to his violin than to his medical studies," recalled Lockhart. The absence of Harold Piper and the evenings spent at the Queen's Hall Roof kept Jenkins away from his old friends.

In July 1920 Edmund Jenkins completed his year of studies with Langrish, ended his studies of the clarinet with Augarde, and was halfway through his harmony course with Corder. He attended the annual prize giving on July 21, 1920, when the prizes were distributed by Lady Cooper, the wife of Sir Edward Cooper, Lord Mayor of London. Cooper was a member of the board of the Royal Academy and had been elected Lord Mayor of London for the year beginning November 1919. An incident that took place about this time, related in 1925, was when Jenkins "chanced to meet with the Lord Mayor in a very busy section of the London streets. His Lordship did Mr. Jenkins the great honor of stopping in the street to inquire after his progress and to shake his hand."[19]

Jenkins had obtained enough money from his private playing to afford a trip to Paris before making his summer journey back home, but he first had to obtain a U.S. passport, which had not been necessary when he had arrived in Britain in May, six years before.

CHAPTER 13

THE REMARKABLE PROGRESS OF THE COLORED POPULATION

In May or June 1920 Edmund Jenkins applied for a passport at the American Embassy in London. Their colleagues in Washington, D.C., cabled on June 18, confirming that Jenkins was indeed a U.S. citizen.[1] On the day after the academy prize giving, Jenkins typed his application. He described himself as a musician, born on April 9, 1894, aged twenty-six, height five feet, six inches, and complexion "negro" (this being typed over a previous entry "black"). He required the passport for a visit to Great Britain and France. Randall Lockhart countersigned to say that he had known Jenkins for three years, giving his address as 24 Goldhurst Terrace, which was the Iles's home in London. Jenkins referred the embassy to his stepmother Eloise Jenkins at 20 Franklin Street, and to Ewin (a typing error for Edwin) Harleston of Calhoun Street, the funeral director. His father must have been away with the orphan band that summer. Issued with U.S. Emergency passport 5289, Edmund Jenkins went to Paris.

Jenkins told something of his journey to readers of *The Academite* 10.

> It was worth the trip to Paris alone to visit the Grand Théâtre Nationale, a truly wonderful building, where I had the pleasure of listening to a performance of "Samson and Delilah," followed, of course, by the inevitable "Ballet." What impressed me most, after the wonderful Opera House structure,

was the precision of technique in the Orchestra, the artistry of the scenic effect, the natural histrionic ability of the actors, and the sympathetic ensemble of the whole. The following points were observed, but, perhaps, in a lesser degree, at L'Opéra Comique.[2]

Jenkins had seen Saint-Saëns's *Samson et Dalila* and the second act of Nuitter and St. Leon's *Coppelia*, both directed by Henri Büsser, on Wednesday, July 28, 1920, at the Opéra.[3] This was a long way from Proctor's Atlanta Festivals when he was at Morehouse College.

Jenkins returned to England from France, and sailed on the *Imperator* from Southampton on Saturday, July 31. He had been paid enough at the Queen's Hall Roof and elsewhere to afford to travel first class, and the register records Edmund Jenkins's address as "c/o Royal Academy, Marylebone Road London" and his occupation as "Ross Scholar."[4] "After calling at Cherbourg in the afternoon of the same day, arrived in New York harbour early in the morning of the 8th of August" continued *The Academite.*

Edmund Jenkins spent one week in New York in mid-August 1920. The city had thousands of black inhabitants, from America's South and from the Caribbean, whose travels were part of the "Great Migration" that was to change American cities in less than twenty years. Along with the rest of America it was impossible to obtain alcoholic refreshment legally. But the change in black America that would have been apparent to Jenkins within hours of leaving the *Imperator* was the black pride expressed by the thousands of followers of the Jamaican Marcus Garvey. Garvey's *Negro World* may have been taken by the Coterie in London, and would certainly have been known and discussed by Jenkins's black friends. Garvey's appeal was to both black Americans and West Indians, and his weekly paper was found—and banned—in many colonial territories. In August 1920 it claimed a fifty-thousand guaranteed circulation.[5] Garvey's Universal Negro Improvement Association (UNIA) had purchased a boat in 1919, and while it was making its second journey to the Caribbean, UNIA purchased a second, to be run by the Black Star Line. On July 20, 1920, the first annual meeting of stockholders was held in New York; this event was overshadowed by the gathering of twenty-five thousand blacks in Madison Square Garden to hear Garvey, on August 2.[6] The black convention continued into the week that Jenkins arrived.

Jenkins had to replace his emergency passport with a proper document, which he did in New York City where white American authority changed his new application form, altering his occupation from "student" to "musician," the description of his chin from "firm" to "round," and his complexion from "dark brown" to "colored." He had no "distinguishing marks" in London in July, but in New York he wrote "man of colour" using the British spelling. His application was countersigned by Paul Daniels, who, not being related, swore an affidavit on August 16, 1920, to say that he had known Jenkins for twenty-six years, that he was a minister, and that he lived at 25 Franklin Street, Charleston, S.C. The official noted his temporary address in Harlem as 251 West 133rd Street, and allowed Daniels to amend his "Edmond" to "Edmund." Jenkins was issued with passport 82560, which was mailed, at Jenkins's request, to 20 Franklin Street. His form said that he would be returning to the United States within twelve months, and that he would be traveling via France and Belgium to England, where he would be studying. His plans to leave New York on the *Aquitania* due to sail on September 22, 1920, were also stated in his application.[7]

Jenkins then went to visit friends in Boston, Mass. In his *Academite* article Jenkins wrote of the distinguished travelers on the *Imperator,* who included Madame Galli Curci of the Metropolitan Opera; Viscount Maitland and his wife; Vincent Astor; Mrs. Vanderbilt and her daughters, and W. T. Tilden, the tennis champion, and members of the Davis Cup Team. "It was quite a coincidence that I should run across Tilden and the Davis Cup Team of Tennis players in Boston, where they were playing matches for the Championship of the United States."[8]

Jenkins's readers of *The Academite* were not likely to be involved with race relations despite their association with him and his black friends. Jenkins's article, therefore, concentrates on musical aspects of America, although he drew in race relations where he could:

> From Boston, returning through New York, I next visited Washington, and on through to Charleston in South Carolina. It was no other than the great composer, Antonin Dvòràk,

who said that the only national music America has consists of
the Negro Folk Music, which the master himself used so effec-
tively and tellingly in his wonderful symphony No. 5 in E
minor and his quartette, both works standing as monumental
testimonials to the truth of his observations (made during his
sojurn in America as principal of the National Conservatoire
of Music). It is, therefore, but natural that I should comment
upon the remarkable progress the coloured population of
America has made, and is still making, in the realms of Art,
as in all other phases of life. This, in spite of the disadvan-
tages to which people of colour are subjected in various forms
and degrees throughout the world—and more especially is it
so, unfortunately, in English-speaking countries. I had a good
opportunity of observing this progress of which I speak in
that, on my way back from Charleston, I visited Columbia,
Greenville (both cities in the state of South Carolina), Atlanta
(in Georgia) and Baltimore (in Maryland). From these places,
along with New York and Boston, I was enabled to get a good
idea as to what was going on generally throughout the
States.[9]

Edmund Jenkins spent about three weeks in Charleston, and, as he
was still there on September 10, his return on the *Aquitania* from
New York twelve days later must have made his journey to Atlanta
rather hurried. Brawley remembered meeting his old friend: "Three
years later he returned. Full of ambition, he begged me to write the
words of an opera for him."[10] Henry Hugh Proctor, in whose
Atlanta church Jenkins had played the cornet, was in New York,
where he was the minister at the Nazarene Congregational Church
in Brooklyn, having traveled to France to help black American
troops there in 1919.[11]

   Jenkins was unable to attend concerts he told the readers of *The
Academite*, for "the short time I spent overseas was in the midst of
the summer period, when not only the concert halls, but even all
theatres, were closed." He was at a concert at his father's church on
Palmetto Street, in the evening of September 9, 1920, when the
"Inner Circle Club" (which was run by the ladies associated with
the orphanage and Parson Jenkins's church—Mrs. Hamilton, Mrs.
Jenkins, Mrs. Dickinson, and Mrs. H. E. Daniels) presented the

contralto Eloise G. Uggams, with Maude H. Smith at the piano in a recital of items including Harry Burleigh's *By An' By*, items by Coleridge-Taylor and Debussy, and an adaption by Miss Smith of *Nobody Knows The Trouble I See*.[12]

Sixty years later Lucius Goggins, former resident of the orphanage and then resident in the Jenkins household at 34 Magazine Street, recalled Edmund Jenkins's playing the piano "day and night" and that the young Jenkins gave a piano recital.[13] As the Uggams and Smith concert was "given in honor of Prof. Edmund T. Jenkins" and was a reception, too, perhaps Jenkins's concert was on another evening.

Six years later E. C. Lockhart of 523 North 10th Street, Fort Smith, Arkansas, wrote to Daniel Jenkins: "During my visit to Charleston about six years ago it was my privilege to see him in all the glory of young manhood. His face showed a peculiar radiance which reflected the artist. His affability was delightful. His English characteristics which were no doubt unconsciously cultivated from contact were superb. He was brilliant, scintillating—bubbling over with music, which seemed to hold his soul captive."[14]

The return voyage on the *Aquitania* included the ship's orchestra, performances of which "proved quite interesting." "A number of Rhodes scholars from Harvard, on their way to Oxford, were aboard ship, and some of them appeared on the programme" of the concert given in aid of the Liverpool Seamen's Orphanage, in which Jenkins contributed "a pianoforte solo of my own composition, with a short piece of Debussy's as an encore, being the only items of an aspiringly classical nature."

"In due course Southampton was reached after making the journey from New York in six days, and from there to London completed a journey of about ten thousand miles."[15]

CHAPTER 14

A HOLD ON
JAZZ IDIOMS

Returning to the Royal Academy of Music at the beginning of
October 1920, Edmund Jenkins started his seventh and final year of
studies with Frederick Corder. His Ross Scholarship paid for the
tuition. His personal file records that he studied harmony with
Corder, voice culture with Thorpe Bates, bassoon and oboe with
E. Fred James, and piano first with Egerton "Bob" Tidmarsh and
later with A. Bush.[1] He continued to edit *The Academite*, with the
Chester brothers and Cynthia Cox. Issue number 10, containing
details of Jenkins's summer trip of 1920, was not only slimmer than
usual, but it was also for both the Michaelmas and Lent terms,
which indicates that Jenkins did not publish a Christmas 1920 issue.

The magazine notes the July 1920 absence of Alexander Mackenzie and his ill-health, operation, and convalescence. Social activities reported include the marriage of Marjorie Perkins to George
Thomson and Thelma Howarth to Captain Basil Machin. Cynthia
Cox described the entertainment to be had while waiting in line for
London concerts and theaters, as buskers "three or four ragged
dirty little urchins with strong voices, active limbs and the famous
London street instrument (made of two spoons, and played something like the bones) . . . treat you to a mixture of ragtime, shuffle-
dancing and jazz." Opposite a page of advertisements for gramophones, priced from £7½ to £70 ($35–$340), is a page of "Guess
Who!" questions, including "Guess who was described as the 'little
dark man who sometimes waves the stick at Orchestral Practices.' "

In London in October 1920 Roland Hayes performed at the Wigmore Hall.[2] On October 19, in Acton, John Barbour-James, who was widowed, married Edith Rita Goring, a mathematics teacher from Barbados. She had been the headmistress of the government girls school in Cape Coast, Gold Coast, and lived in Camberwell, the area where Harold Moody had his medical practice.[3] One of the witnesses was A. S. Cann.[4]

Herbert Henry of the Queen's Hall had continued to negotiate with Behar in Paris for clarinets and other items while Jenkins had been in America. The clarinets left Paris on October 6, 1920, and Jenkins obtained the shipping documents and paid the import duty.[5] Jenkins also had Behar's letter to Henry, whose wife did not translate the letter (if her title "Madame Henri" justifies the suggestion that she was French), which also referred to "toiles." This was translated as "linen" but should have been translated as theater curtains or drapes. Jenkins and Henry were working together to convert the Queen's Hall small hall into a proper musical night club, to be decorated with curtains imported from France, and to be run by a company incorporated on November 25, 1920, as the Q S H Syndicate Limited with Herbert Henry as one of the four directors.[6]

Bert Bassett, an experienced banjo player who had recorded for the Jumbo label before the war, had worked with Harry Robbins, Sr., and Dick De Pauw, a violinist, in London in 1917. These three were probably the original members of the band, with Ivy and Jenkins, when Hylton joined in late 1919. The trumpeter by the beginning of 1921 was a south Londoner, Harold "Bert" Heath, who had been brought up, with his trombone-playing brother George "Ted" Heath, in the brass band tradition. Ted Heath was part of a street busking band, and he remembered this period in his autobiography.

> Our busking band often played outside the Queen's Hall Roof Garden, in Langham Place, London, a meeting place of the swells and about the most fashionable night club in those days. My brother Harold played the trumpet there. He'd wave a greeting to me though we were professionally poles apart.[7]

Heath recalled being introduced to "the relief pianist" of the band, Jack Hylton, who asked him to substitute for their regular trombonist who was ill. The ten pounds a week salary was a "small fortune," but Heath only lasted four nights since the subtleties of jazz phrasing were a complete mystery to him.

"Harold gave me another push. The upshot was that Jenkins, the coloured saxophonist who led the Roof Gardens band, introduced me to the manager of an all-coloured American jazz band that was shortly to leave London for an engagement in Vienna. The Southern Syncopated Orchestra was short of a trombonist and a trumpet player."[8]

The time may be somewhat different than Ted Heath recalled. He probably played for four days in 1921, but the Vienna trip with Lattimore's orchestra may have been in 1922.[9] The trombonist in the band in the small hall on the roof was Jesse Stamp, one of the classically trained musicians known to Jenkins from his years of work in London's orchestras. In 1921 the group listened to a record that "Mme. Henri" had brought back from her trip to New York in late 1920.[10] Hylton remembered later that this recording led to a dispute when he suggested that the orchestra, Paul Whiteman's, was playing from music. "Fortunately, Jenkins, whose voice carried weight on all musical matters, confirmed my opinion."[11] Hylton arranged to copy Whiteman's orchestrations, which would make the band the most modern in London.

On May 28, 1921, the band went to the Hayes, Middlesex, studios of His Master's Voice (HMV), the British associate of Victor, and recorded four tunes. They were paid five pounds each.[12] The eight musicians were Bert Heath (trumpet), Jesse Stamp (trombone), Bert Worth (alto saxophone), Edmund Jenkins (clarinet and alto saxophone), Dick De Pauw (violin), Jack Hylton (piano and celesta), Bert Bassett (banjo), and Wag Abbey (drums). The arrangements of these four tunes seem to have few similiarities to Paul Whiteman's American recordings.

The four recordings were issued on two double-sided ten-inch discs, numbered B-1236 and B-1237. The choice of tune shows the dance-band nature of the group, for two were fox trots, one was a waltz, and the other a quick-step. The first tune recorded was *Idol of Mine*, composed by Pollack and featuring Jenkins playing the saxophone, with a slide or swannee whistle solo. Abbey was restricted to part of the drum kit, as any sound would be recorded by the apparatus which was acoustic: a sudden loud beat would make the apparatus jump. The rhythmic approach of the band

5. The "Queen's" Dance Orchestra at the HMV studios, Hayes, Middlesex, May 28, 1921. *Courtesy Brian Rust, Hatch End, Middlesex.*

shows why it attracted the "swells" of London in 1921.

The second composition recorded that day was *Turque.* It took two attempts to get the version that was issued on B-1236. The piece was composed by Paul Wyer and Pierre de Caillaux, both members of the Southern Syncopated Orchestra. Wyer had worked with W. C. Handy before World War I, and would have been known to Jenkins before Hylton left Lancashire in late 1919. Jenkins's clarinet trills above the orchestra in a military band style and is clearer than the other instruments, perhaps a result of the musicians' positions around the recording horn.

Betty Boutelle's *The Wind in the Trees* was issued with *Idol of Mine* on B-1237. It starts with Jenkins's saxophone, with Worth's saxophone, and De Pauw's violin, and they are joined by trumpet and trombone. A "wind" effect is created by the swannee whistle. A saxophone, probably Jenkins's, has two short breaks, followed by one from the banjo and one from Hylton's piano, concluding with ensemble.

The partner to *Turque* on B-1236 was Hylton's *I'm Wondering If It's Love,* a waltz introduced by the violin. The swannee whistle plays the melody against Hylton's celesta (toy piano). Jenkins plays the saxophone, but there is nothing of note in his work.

The band returned to the studio on July 8, 1921, but without Bert Worth. Four tunes were recorded, to be issued on HMV's cheaper label "Zonophone" under the name *Jack Hylton's Jazz Band* instead of the previous *"Queen's" Dance Orchestra.* The first tune the group recorded was *The Love Nest,* by the American composer Louis Hirsch, whose works had been played by Jenkins at the Anglo-American Exposition in July 1914. This tune had been recorded by Tony Tuck with the Versatile Three for the Winner label in December 1920. Three attempts were made to get an acceptable version, and the third "take" was issued on Zonophone 2155. Jenkins's alto saxophone is featured playing the melody, followed by the verse. His saxophone then plays what appears to be an improvised solo, with trombone breaks from Stamp and, finally, Heath. It is dance music, not jazz.

The other side of Zonophone 2155 is Maurice Yvain's *Mon Homme (My Man).* Jenkins plays the saxophone. Bassett's rhythm is excellent, and so is Jenkins's obbligato solo. The band had three attempts at this tune, too. The third was issued.

The two other tunes recorded were issued on Zonophone 2167,

with *Billy* by "West and Hylton" recorded satisfactorily the first time. Bassett's shuffle-rhythm is the most notable part of this recording, which ends with Jenkins playing a fast run over the band's coda.

The other side of *Billy* is *Wang Wang Blues*, which was written by Busse, Mueller, and Johnson, the trumpet, clarinet and trombone players in Whiteman's orchestra. The band played Whiteman's classic arrangement well, leaving plenty of room for Jenkins's clarinet, sounding like Larry Shields in the last chorus. A perceptive commentator on black culture was later to write: "As a child, Jenkins had been a member of his father's Charleston (South Carolina) Orphanage Band and had acquired a hold on Negro idioms and jazz accent that persisted after years abroad following his graduation from the London Royal College [*sic*] of Music."[13] The similarity between the 1917 and 1919 recordings of the clarinet of New Orleans-born white Larry Shields and the 1921 recordings of Charleston-born black Edmund Jenkins may point to a common root in American folk music.

The band was photographed in the studio, an improvement on the previous souvenir, a sketch by De Pauw which showed Bert Worth without shoes—probably to approach the recording horn without making too much noise—and with holes in his socks.[14]

Shortly after this session at Hayes, Edmund Jenkins completed his studies at the Royal Academy of Music. He was elected an Associate of the Royal Academy of Music (ARAM), a distinguished honor. He had been subprofessor (clarinet). He had completed courses in the study of harmony, composition, voice, the clarinet, the oboe, the bassoon, the organ, and the piano. He was also able to play the cornet, the trombone, the various horns, the violin, the bass clarinet, the alto saxophone and was able to compose for full orchestra, to arrange choral music, and to orchestrate songs.

He moved to 108 Lauderdale Mansions, a fine apartment block off Maida Vale in a prosperous area of London near to the Paddington home of John and Minnie Alcindor and their three boys. Mimi Durkin sent him a postcard in July 1921 from her home, Palling, on the eastern coast of England near Yarmouth, and she suggested to Jenkins that he should "come to Y'mouth with Harry we will get over to see you."[15]

6. Frederick Corder, ca. 1921. Original photograph taken by Edmund Jenkins. *From a negative in the possession of the late Edwina Fleming of Charleston, S.C.*

During July and August 1921 many of Jenkins's black friends had been gathering in London for a meeting of the Pan-African Congress to be held at the Central Hall in Westminster. NAACP leaders Du Bois, Walter White, and Jessie Fauset joined John Barbour-James, Robert Broadhurst, John Eldred Taylor, and Roland Hayes at the gathering. The 113 delegates had expected the meeting to be opened by the French black politician Blaise Diagne, but Dr. John Alcindor, chairman of the African Progress Union, opened the meeting on Saturday, August 27, 1921. Others attending that session, or the second, which was on Monday, August 29, included Jenkins's acquaintances and friends F. W. Dove, John Archer, American entertainer Creighton Thompson's wife, Lawrence Brown the pianist, and Mrs. Coleridge-Taylor.[16] Although no evidence has been found to show that Jenkins attended the meetings, he was certainly in London that weekend, for the band's next appointment in Hayes was on Tuesday, August 30th. Du Bois had written to Jenkins at the Royal Academy from New York on June 18, 1921, and by the end of September Jenkins was involved with Du Bois, Broadhurst, and Alcindor. It seems likely that Edmund Jenkins was one of the audience at this conference.

The Pan-African Congress was very much the work of Du Bois and the NAACP, who had joined with Taylor and Archer in Paris in early 1919 and whose contacts were renewed in the summer of 1921 by Robert Broadhurst and an exmissionary John Harris, who had concerned themselves with African affairs for many years. Harris had been interviewed in 1905 and the results, published in the London *Review of Reviews* in September, 1905, were added to Mark Twain's condemnation of the atrocities in the Congo under King Leopold, *King Leopold's Soliloquy.* Other worthies who had condemned this exploitation included Arthur Conan Doyle (the creator of Sherlock Holmes) and Edmund Morel, an associate of the socialist George Lansbury. Harris had become the secretary of the Anti-Slavery and Aborigines Protection Society in London. He was involved in the antiimperial world of the Fisher Unwin group and had been helping Plaatje. He was at the dinner party of the African Progress Union and had been secretary of the Committee for the Welfare of Africans in Europe, with which Audrey Jeffers had also worked.[17]

The gathering in London included a number of Africans from

Gambia, Sierra Leone, Nigeria, and the Gold Coast. On Sunday, August 28, 1921, when there was no official meeting, some of the group may have gathered in Jenkins's new apartment in Lauderdale Mansions.

Jenkins's socialist friend John Archer introduced the communist Labour candidate for the Battersea parliamentary constituency, who was an Indian, Shapurji Saklatvala. He told the gathering that India supported them. Saklatvala was to be Member of Parliament for Battersea even when he stood without Labour Party support. His effect on the mainly black audience was quite different than the "rapid, heated utterances of Mr. B. E. Varma, a member of the Indian Delegation at present in London, who spoke in the evening."[18] Alcindor said that "the African's worst enemy was the African who lacked character, education, and cohesion."[19] The congress had been arranged at short notice and had no program.[20] It owed a lot to Du Bois's reactions to the black support for Garvey, whose second International Convention of Negroes of the World was held in New York in August 1921. The congress moved to Brussels and met from August 30 until September 2, and then moved to Paris. Although Jenkins did not join Du Bois and the others who went to Belgium, his wealth, associations, and ambitions must have involved him in this London gathering.

The recording session of August 30, 1921, resulted in the *"Queen's" Dance Orchestra* appearing on three 78 rpm discs. They only recorded four tunes, since two of the discs had one side pressed from American recordings of Victor. The orchestra with Jenkins playing fox trots played on both sides of HMV B-1258. *Ilo (A Voice from Mummyland)* had been written by Johnny Black, whose *Dardanella* had been a tremendously popular tune. The second take was issued. *Ilo* starts with a cymbal beat from Abbey. The banjo is excellent, the violin is inaccurate, and Jenkins's saxophone is not very interesting. The melody has reminders of Black's earlier hit. The breaks are taken by Jenkins, Bassett, Heath, Stamp, followed by an excellent violin break, and Hylton's piano.

The other side of HMV B-1258 is a medley entitled *So Now You Know*, introducing *Billy*, both by Hylton. Three attempts were made at this recording session to get an acceptable version of this and both of the other two tunes. The orchestra starts, and Jenkins and the violin (De Pauw?) play a duet. The saxophone then plays a fast run through the octave, followed by ensemble. Then Jenkins plays an improvised chorus against the brass and the violin. The swannee whistle follows, against a fussy brass chorus, emphasizing Jenkins as the main soloist with the band, and also his feeling and flair for playing the new syncopated dance music.

HMV B-1259 was issued with R. Stolz's *Oriental Fox Trot—Salome* by the roof orchestra, backed with the Benson Orchestra of Chicago playing Rose's fox trot *I'll Keep On Loving You. Salome* has Jenkins playing the alto saxophone and the bass clarinet, which led the recording magazine *The Voice* of October 1921 to report on "the instrument which gives the startling effects in 'Salome' " and "It is a bass clarinet which supplies the comic effect." The same magazine in September 1921 had a photograph of the band, and the saxophone player is neither Jenkins nor Worth. *Salome's* Oriental flavor is in the tango rhythm implied in the melody. Jenkins has to change from saxophone, which he plays over Hylton and Bassett's firm rhythm, to bass clarinet, which plays breaks with Stamp and then with Heath. Jenkins returns to the saxophone and plays strongly, possibly with relief.

The last of the four tunes recorded on August 30, 1921, was *Campañas*, which was described as a *Bell Fox Trot* on the label of HMV B-1262. It was composed by Pastallé and Viladomat. The other side, by the *All Star Trio* of saxophone, xylophone, and piano, was Bowman's *Twelfth Street Rag. Campañas* has a bell introduction, and Jenkins plays the saxophone against Bassett's banjo. Jenkins then changes to the clarinet for a chorus, interrupted by two "laughing trombone" breaks by Stamp. More bell-like sounds from the piano and drums are followed by a stilted but accurate solo from Jenkins's alto saxophone. When the entire orchestra plays, the saxophone plays a fast and free-flowing obbligato. Stamp and Jenkins play a break in unison, and then the bells are heard. Jenkins's saxophone concludes the recording.

Dr. Alcindor and the APU attended a special dinner in early August at the Savoy Hotel in London with Chief Oluwa of Lagos and his assistant Herbert Macaulay.[21] In late July the London press had noted the arrival from America of J. E. K. Aggrey. Aggrey had left his native Gold Coast in 1898, and, having considered studying in Colwyn Bay,[22] he had lived in North Carolina for more than twenty years. He was traveling to Africa to investigate education prospects in the areas of British domination, and he probably stayed with John Barbour-James.[23] Roland Hayes was performing at the Queen's Hall Promenade Concert on September 8, and at the Wigmore Hall on September 24.[24] The south African John L. Dube was in London and writing to John Harris in late September.[25] Since Alcindor was invited to the Pan-African Congress by Harris, it seems likely that Dube was present at Portman Rooms in London on the night of Thursday, September 29, when the APU "at very short notice" had arranged a reception and dance in honor of Du Bois. This APU reception was reported in various magazines as well as in the *African World* "West African Supplement" to the issue of September 30, 1921, which says, "The organisers are Dr. John Alcindor, Chairman of the African Progress Union, Mr. Robert Broadhurst, Hon. Secretary of the Union, and Secretary for England of the Pan-African Congress, and Mr. Edmund T. Jenkins." Du Bois arrived in London by airplane from Paris only a few hours before the reception.

On October 4, 1921, Roland Hayes was again at the Queen's Hall Promenade Concerts; his friend Jenkins was probably upstairs entertaining the guests at Henry's night club. Earlier that day the band had been back to the recording studio and had three attempts at Ivy St. Helier's *Coal Black Mammy*. All three were rejected, but, probably in error, the first take appears on some copies of Zonophone 2191, which also has the first take of this tune, which the band recorded on October 12. The October 4 session was rather unsuccessful, for there were three attempts at *Mooning*, and three at a recent Irving Berlin tune entitled *Beautiful Faces*. None of the six attempts was issued. The only recording from the October 4 session that was issued officially was *A Trombone Cocktail*, a one-step written by Stamp.

A Trombone Cocktail was issued on HMV B-1276. It is the fastest tempo recording the band had made. Jenkins played the alto saxophone, but the recording features Jesse Stamp's trombone. Bassett demonstrated his mastery of the banjo by playing just two strings, which gives a bounce to the band.

On October 8, Roland Hayes and Lawrence Brown gave a recital at the Wigmore Hall, in aid of the African Progress Union.[26] Since it was held in the afternoon, Edmund Jenkins was probably in the audience.

The black and musical friends of Jenkins suffered a tragic loss with the sinking of the *Rowan* on the night of October 9, 1921. The Southern Syncopated Orchestra of Lattimore was traveling from Glasgow to play at the Scala Theater in Dublin when their ship suffered two collisions crossing the Irish Sea. Sidney Bechet's autobiography says that the band lost all their instruments and confirmed that eight musicians died. By the time of this accident he had left the group to work in a dance band touring England, and, therefore, lacked firsthand information; newspaper reports from England and Scotland are confusing. Other blacks had joined the SSO replacing Bechet and others. One of the victims was Frank Lacton, from Sierra Leone, whose body was washed ashore on October 18. The funeral was arranged by the black community of Glasgow.[27] Evelyn Dove and Mrs. King Reavis were not injured, and neither were three Africans, William Ofori of the Gold Coast, F. Kennedy from Sierra Leone, and Guy Martins from Nigeria, still recovering from their ordeal according to *West Africa* of October 29, 1921.

John Alexander Barbour-James's son, an amateur organist and pianist, is reported to have died about this time, and he may have been on the *Rowan*.[28]

On October 12 the band returned to the HMV recording studios and had two more attempts at *Coal Black Mammy*. Both were issued, each on different labels. The first take was issued on Zonophone 2191 under the *Jack Hylton's Jazz Band* title. This disc also has the first take of the October 4 session, pressed by mistake.

The October 4 version is faster than those of October 12, and Jenkins's alto saxophone is different, especially in the first chorus. Bert Heath's trumpet is different, too, and so is the recording balance. Jenkins's bass clarinet is clearer on the later recording session. The second take of *Coal Black Mammy*, being slightly better, was issued on the higher-priced HMV label, on B-1275, under the *"Queen's" Dance Orchestra* title. The three issued versions of this one tune all end with fast alto saxophone from Jenkins, the October 4 session being faster and more skilled.

Mooning, which had been a failure three times on October 4, was also recorded twice on October 12. The first attempt was better and was issued on HMV B-1275. The second attempt at Hylton's fox trot was released on Zonophone 2191. The problem in these recordings is the fussy arrangement, which necessitated Jenkins changing from alto saxophone to bass clarinet and back. As the noise of the dancers in the Queen's Hall Roof Club tended to drown a quiet instrument like the bass clarinet, the recording arrangement may have been different from the usual performances. The coda on *Coal Black Mammy* was probably part of the band's normal version, since it features Jenkins playing very fast through two bars of *Dixie*.

Mooning has Jenkins playing the saxophone, with the swannee whistle playing while Jenkins changes to the bass clarinet. Jenkins changes back during a short bridge and demonstrates his abilities and technical mastery of the saxophone. The two versions recorded on October 12 have slightly different performances by the saxophone and bass clarinet, but not in any marked way. The HMV issue is of higher quality than the Zonophone.

The last tune recorded by the band on October 12 was T. V. Norman's fox trot *Counting the Days*. The first take was issued on HMV B-1276 with *A Trombone Cocktail* of October 4. Jenkins's alto saxophone is played with some vibrato, and he changes to the clarinet. The sound is reminiscent of the clarinet of Larry Shields in the ODJB recordings of 1917 and 1919.

The band went back to the Hayes studio on October 18. The violinist on all previous recordings had been of little note, but from this date it seems to be a different musician, possibly Johnny Rosen. The old group had tried Hylton's *So Now You Know* three times on August 30, and the third attempt had been issued on HMV B-1258. The October 18 version, released on Zonophone 2223, has Heath's trumpet playing a duet with Jenkins, and not the violin and saxophone duet of August.

All four tunes recorded on October 18, 1921, were issued under Hylton's name on Zonophone. The reverse side of *So Now You Know* is *Tsing*, a composition by J. Derrick. His composition sounds similar to the dixieland jazz band favorite *That's a Plenty*. It is a one-step, in a military band style. Jenkins plays the clarinet. There is an Oriental mood to the tune, which also has a "jazzy" feel, perhaps from the tune's associations. The new violinist is much better than De Pauw.

The other two tunes recorded that day were both played twice before a version suitable for public sale was cut. They were issued on Zonophone 2199, earlier than the other pair on Zonophone

2223. Jesse Stamp had written *Laughing Waltz* with Hylton, and the tune features Stamp's "laughing" trombone, backed by violin and alto saxophone. Jenkins then plays the saxophone for one chorus, interrupted by the band's shouting "Ho, Ho, Ho!" Hylton's celesta or toy piano, plays behind Stamp, and the recording ends with a low bass note from Stamp.

The other side of Zonophone 2199 is Walter Donaldson's 1920 composition *My Mammy*. Jenkins plays the alto saxophone with a considerable vibrato, perhaps the influence of Bechet, whose vibrato was extreme, or perhaps because Jenkins was no longer concerned with a pure classical tone. It is possible to play the clarinet with an orthodox tone, and the saxophone with a vibrato; Jenkins's playing on *My Mammy* may be just due to his getting used to the saxophone. There appears to be a brass bass on this recording, but this is uncertain because of the pre-electric recording and the quality and condition of the shellac disc, pressed in 1921. Dance bands in the early 1920s generally interspersed one song with snatches of others. *My Mammy* includes Bert Heath playing *Wait Til the Sun Shines, Nellie*. The record ends with Jenkins playing his fast and technique-displaying run on the saxophone.

The band went to the studios for a fourth time in October 1921, recording three waltzes and a fox trot on October 27. Two of the waltzes were attributed to London music entrepreneurs, one to Herman Darewski and the other to Horatio Nicholls (also known as Lawrence Wright). Entrepreneurs bought songs from unknown composers and issued them, through their own publishing companies, under their own names. When a record or song sold well, they benefited from their enterprise. Composers tended to have jaundiced opinions of this type of activity, of course. Two saxophones played on these recordings; the alto saxophone that accompanied the trumpet on *Circulation* is Jenkins. Darewski's second composition issued on HMV B-1286 was the fox trot *Gossiping*. The arrangement is complicated, and Jenkins switches from the saxophone to the clarinet. The violinist is different than on the pre-September recordings. If it is Rosen, it is understandable why Hylton employed him in the late 1920s.

The other disc from this session was HMV B-1287, which had Nicholls's waltz *Silver Star* featuring Heath's trumpet. The third chorus has two saxophones, with celesta at the end, which continues with the violin. Heath repeats the rather sweet melody. This tune may have been a regular feature at Langham Place, for the band completed a satisfactory version at the first attempt.

Charles L. Johnson's waltz *Sweet and Low* was recorded after two attempts. It is lively, has a fuller sound than the earliest recordings by the band, perhaps a result of the extra saxophone and the positioning of the players around the recording horn, but more likely because of greater experience and better writing for two reeds. Jenkins plays the clarinet.

Roland Hayes was appearing at the Wigmore Hall on November 11, 1921.[29] On November 15 the band returned to the HMV recording studios and had three more attempts at Berlin's *Beautiful Faces Need Beautiful Clothes*. This fox trot was issued on HMV B-1298, with a one-step *Why?* written by Hylton's wife Ennis Parkes on the other side. Both feature Jenkins playing the alto saxophone, with *Why?*'s fussy arrangement leading to Jenkins playing in an unrestricted style.

The other two tunes were issued after one playing. HMV B-1299 had two one-steps. The unknown J. Derrick wrote *Come Along*, which, as on his *Tsing*, features Jenkins on the clarinet. It has a fast tempo, perhaps too fast for comfort, but even at this speed Jenkins makes no false steps. There are echoes of military bands and the ODJB.

Come Along was the last tune recorded that day. Jerome Kern's *The Bull Frog Patrol* was issued on the other side of B-1299. This is a fine tune, and this version may be the earliest on disc. Jenkins plays the clarinet throughout, while Stamp plays the "frog" noises on the trombone. Yet again Jenkins's playing is reminiscent of Larry Shields, but there can be no questioning that Edmund Jenkins was a master of the clarinet. The record shows the quality that attracted the swells of London to the Queen's Hall Roof and made Edmund Jenkins one of the wealthiest musicians in London. Harry Leekam remembered his salary as fifty pounds a week, and a 1926 New York newspaper report refers to "a stipend of $75 a week."[30] The band had an argument, and Jenkins left some time between November 15, 1921, and their next recording date of February 13, 1922, when the discs included the phrase "directed by Jack Hylton." Jenkins is on neither the clarinet nor saxophone after November 1921.

Hylton wrote in 1939 "things went on merrily and then an event of seeming unimportance, but of far-reaching consequence to me, occurred in the sudden decision of Jenkins, our coloured clarinettist, to leave us."[31] Hylton replaced Jenkins with a black saxophonist named Dixon who was playing at the Embassy Club. Dixon and Hylton had an argument, and Hylton left for a while, probably about May to July 1922.[32] Jenkins may have been expressing his dissatisfaction with the band during late 1921, for the January 1922 edition of *The Dancing Life* comments: "When is the native saxophonist of the Queen's Hall Dance Orchestra 'going back,' as he so repeatedly tells us it is his intention so to do?"[33]

The same magazine noted the numbers of foreigners in dance bands, commenting that "The 'darkie' question, as it concerns dance orchestras, seems to be getting still darker." Its emphasis is on patriotism, not music: "Everybody knows that Englishmen can play every bit as well as South Americans, and sometimes better, and I confess that it always annoys me to see a coloured orchestra playing when there is so much English talent available." By South American the writer meant Americans from the southern states, which was an association that Will Marion Cook had noted when he named his 1919 orchestra in London. The part played in the new music in America by black Americans was to lead Louis Hirsch to write *It's Getting Dark on Old Broadway*.

Jenkins had been involved with the dance band at Henry's night club for two years, and his dispute with Hylton may have been just one of the reasons he left. He went from London to Paris, first calling on Winifred Small and later, from Paris, mailing her a pair of white kid leather gloves.[34]

CHAPTER 15

ONE OF THE CHIC DANCING PLACES IN PARIS

Edmund Jenkins had expressed his wish to travel to France and Belgium when completing his passport application in New York in August 1920. Since he was a well-known musician in London, recording for HMV, and talented in the new music, it was likely that French or Belgian businessmen would recognize his abilities at the Queen's Hall Roof and make offers for this black American to lead a group at their latest night spot. Arthur Briggs of the SSO spent most of the rest of his life in Europe, working with Salnave in Belgium, and recording in Berlin in 1927. Frank Withers who also had played at the Coterie Coleridge-Taylor concert was later to work with Bechet in Soviet Russia. Paul Wyer worked in London and then South America, John C. Payne in London until the 1930s, and other SSO members in France, Spain, and Scandinavia. It was from the Mediterranean resort of Monte Carlo that Jenkins received a letter from Ted Toiros, dated January 16, 1922, which replied to a letter from Jenkins. It said "Regarding Acacias, I will write to Molyneux now and see what he has to offer for a band and also the dancing end. I have had a tough battle here about you as I want you to come down here to the Cafe de Paris." The writer asked Jenkins how much he wanted for a band: "not too good because they wont pay and what is the *least* you will take alone. It will be a good holiday if you need one." Acacias was a night club at 49 rue des Acacias in Paris[1] and it may be presumed from this letter the Edmund Jenkins was in Paris at the beginning of 1922.

In November 1925, following an interview with Jenkins in the

United States, the American black monthly *Opportunity* said that Jenkins's move to Paris was:

> In response to an offer from Art Hickman's Orchestra, a band of white Americans who played first in London, and afterwards in Paris. They were in need of a clarinet and saxophone player, and, having heard of his triumphs in London, telegraphed an offer of two thousand francs. In those days this was a salary well up in the hundreds of dollars in American currency, and Art Hickman's Orchestra is one of America's leading dance orchestras, ranking favorably with those of Vincent Lopez and Paul Whiteman. They played at the Ermitage de Longes Champs in the Bois de Boulogne, one of the most *chic* of Paris' tea and night dancing places.[2]

In the show business world of dance bands the work of early pioneers has been overshadowed by their imitators who rose to international success. Art Hickman, a white band leader from California, contributed the saxophone to dance bands. The sound that his band made was so popular that a band calling itself Art Hickman's New York London Five, worked and recorded in London in 1920 without Hickman, who probably never left America.[3] Hickman's saxophone star was Bert Ralton, who left Hickman in 1919 and traveled to London via Cuba. He was in London by the middle of 1922,[4] but the undocumented activities of dance bands and the self-promotion of the leaders make it impossible to say which musician in the Hickman band in Paris had created the vacancy that Jenkins filled.

Harry Leekam recalled an incident affecting his brother and Jenkins, who had been playing at a night club in Birkenhead. He reported to Dr. Tony Martin that, after he had returned to his studies in London, his brother and Jenkins "had a close shave— Jenkins drove the car in which they were driving right through the gate of a farm. The road had curved suddenly and he didn't realise it in time. Luckily there were no serious injuries."[5] The incident may have led to a claim by the farmer, for Randall Lockhart wrote to Jenkins in Paris in early August 1922:

> You asked me to find out if your case had been heard; I imagine you to have meant the accident case; because there

would be, so far as I understand, no case with Mrs. Dove, no
writ or anything having been served on you. In the other
case, you would be the defendant; but as I did not know the
name of the plaintiff, I could not find out, especially as I did
not know when you thought the case likely to be heard.

Jenkins had purchased a car in Britain in 1921, paying £695
($3,500), a considerable sum for that period. His Talbot Darracq
was one of the fastest cars of its type, and three times the price of a
more modest family car. The incident recalled by Dr. Leekam in
1980 may not be the accident that Lockhart's letter mentions, and it
also has to be guessed that Mrs. Dove was one of the Sierra Leone
Doves, possibly Evelyn Dove's (by now Mrs. Luke) mother.[6]

Jenkins was in France for the first half of 1922, but still in contact
with his Caribbean friends. Percy Acham-Chen, the law student
from Trinidad, had completed his studies and had traveled to Paris.
From his London home, 12 Boundary Road, St. John's Wood,
which was not far from Lauderdale Mansions in Maida Vale, Percy
wrote to Jenkins to thank him for his hospitality during their recent
get-together in Paris. He also told Jenkins that the family was
returning to Port of Spain shortly and that Harry and Mimi
Leekam were going to the Channel Island of Jersey to study for his
October final examinations. "I hope he gets through as his arrival
with Mrs. Leekam will swell the crowd in Trinidad." He also asked
Jenkins "how is the car going," which confirms that Jenkins's car
was in Paris, and concludes, "Hope you have great success at
l'Ermitage as Chef d'orchestre. Write and let us know what is hap-
pening. Thanks again for your kindness in Paris."[7]

Agatha Acham-Chen also wrote to thank Jenkins for his consideration towards Percy and Sylvia in Paris and gave her Trinidad
home address so that the old friends could keep in touch.

Jenkins took over the Ermitage orchestra, and the 1925 report in
Opportunity reported "Today Art Hickman is gone, and in his
stead reigns Mr. Jenkins as conductor of a thirteen-man dance
orchestra made up entirely of Frenchmen!"[8] Documents found in
Charleston in 1979 include an undated letter from "Binnie" written
from the Hotel de Madrid, 1 rue Geoffroy Main, Paris. It refers to
"one man in a very large place here, a Russian place, which looks
very smart" and suggests that Jenkins come to Paris, to form a
band: "it appears to me that there might be a chance if one had a

band. If there is any mail for me address it here, and oblige—also Jenkins I heard that Haston wanted a drummer. Will you call him up at once NORTH 1480—and tell him I have no Band, and will be pleased to join him if he so desires and the inducements are OK." Gus Haston's London telephone number, references to Jenkins being "comfortable in the flat," and mention of a razor strop at the end of the bed indicate that Binnie was a flatmate of Jenkins at 108 Lauderdale Mansions, had traveled to Paris in the fall of 1921, and, out of work, wanted Jenkins to join him in Paris to form a group with Binnie on drums, to play at the "Russian place." L'Ermitage would be a white Russian cafe or restaurant, one of the hundreds of businesses run in Paris in the 1920s by anti-Soviet Russians in exile.

Jenkins was back in London in late July 1922. The Royal Academy of Music was celebrating its first one hundred years and gave a series of concerts at the Duke's Hall and at the Queen's Hall. Jenkins, as an honored exstudent (the ARAM was not awarded lightly) was invited to join the celebrations, and at the Queen's Hall in the afternoon of July 18, 1922, he played the bass clarinet in the orchestra of one hundred. Augarde played the clarinet; the 'cellos included John Barbirolli and Doris Griffiths, and two of the five horns were A. E. Brain and Francis Bradley. Wilfred James played the bassoon, and John Solomon, who had been giving trumpet lessons to Arthur Briggs, was the principal trumpet.[9] Not playing that afternoon, but playing later in the week of celebrations, was Jesse Stamp.[10]

Jenkins's visit to London was very short. Randall Lockhart was living at 8 Vivian Gardens in Wembley Hill, some distance along the railway line from Maida Vale, when he started a letter to "My dear Jenks" on July 30, 1922, mentioning "the way in which you treated me when you just went to Paris." Lockhart had been unable to meet Jenkins in London as he had no money for fare. "I am sorry, for I would have liked to have seen you, and how gay Paree agrees with you. I imagine you must be thoroughly gallicised by now." Lockhart started the letter again a few days later, and wrote ten pages in a close handwriting.

> I am much interested to learn of the opportunities for social commerce that you have; and pleased for yourself and because of my liking and regard for the French, to hear that you are finding your stay as pleasant as you anticipated.

Lockhart noted "the stiff hours of work that you have," and that:

> Last Friday I saw Percy Acham, and he told me what a pleas-
> ant time his sister and he had in Paris, a good deal of the
> pleasantness being owed to you. I gathered from that that you
> found a little time to frequent Montmartre and to dance. By
> the way, he told me of an offer that you have received to
> become at the close of the present season, a chef d'orchestre of
> the place where you are now. I asked him whether it would be
> a large orchestra and whether you would be doing serious
> music. To which he replied that he believed the other mem-
> bers of the present band would be got rid of, and that you
> would have the choice of doing what you chose. That's excel-
> lent news, i'faith; if I understood him correctly.

Lockhart's use of old English reflects his legal studies which were
shortly to come to an end. His regard for the French came from his
education in Martinique, but he may have had a large French influence in his background, for his planter father A. R. C. Lockhart of
Dominica had given him the French middle name of Hippolyte.

Lockhart had noted, over the five years that he had known
Edmund Jenkins, a change in his ambitions and character. The
twenty-two-year-old Lockhart viewed Jenkins's way of life with
concern; Edmund Jenkins had a large income from playing dance
music, owned a fast car, and was popular at dance establishments
of the highest fashion in London and Paris.

> It is with great concern that I noticed the thinning of the
> chances of you beginning the work which was your first
> ambition (your only ambition, for since you partly aban-
> doned it, you had desires but your ambitious bump had de-
> creased, if you will forgive me saying it). It is not only because
> I temperamentally prefer the idealistic to the practical, but
> out of love and regard for you: I have always felt, Jenks, that
> you never had that happiness, and the feeling of purposeful-
> ness as in the days when you had little money and many
> ideals, little acquisitions and worldly experience, and much
> religious faith and moral earnestness.

Lockhart had told Piper, back in Trinidad, of their friend's changed attitudes, and, enclosing Piper's latest letter, Lockhart commented that "He has some remarks on the subject. I hope we are friends enough for you not to take offence. I wrote him telling him of your movements; and of the large income you were carving, and added that I thought it a pity you should have relinquished your original plans on that account."

Lockhart told Jenkins of the latest news he had on their mutual friends. "I have not seen Escallier or the Leekams since you left. I had from Mrs. Hughes the news of the death of Leekam's father." Lockhart had heard that Ferdie Leekam and Escallier had gone to Brighton for a week's vacation. Harry Leekam was awaiting the results of his examination. The Acham-Chens were leaving England on August 12: "Methinks some rumour reached me of you developing a great deal of interest in the family; it would appear that you consider you cannot have too many irons in the fire." Lockhart had seen the Iles family "I am sorry for Mrs. Iles; they are all going through rather hard times." "I saw the Andrews once for a short time. Harry is still hopeful and talking big; it would seem that some responsible Trinidad firms are interested in the idea which may even get Government support or encouragement." Harry Andrews and his wife were in business in London.

Lockhart's long letter also refers to his father's wish that he should practice law in the West Indies. Randall Lockhart thought that Trinidad would be the best place. He expressed doubts as to his activities after he qualified, and then considered Edmund Jenkins's position in France.

> I suppose that under present circumstances you will feel like staying on in France. I, in your place, would want to; and indeed I am making up my mind that if after going to settle in the W. Indies or in W. Africa, I return to Europe on a holiday visit, I shall not come to England.

Lockhart said that he would try to get to Paris after he completed his examinations. He told Jenkins that a French girl, who had stayed at the same Wembley Hill house for a month to improve her English, had been visited by her lawyer father. He had suggested to Lockhart that he take legal studies in Paris, and thus became qualified to work on matters subject to both English and French legal systems, with obvious commercial advantages. Lockhart told Jenkins that his main interest in the idea was to get away from British culture and expressed a love of French culture.

On the final page of his ten-page letter Lockhart asked Jenkins to try to contact a Martinique family in Paris, and "My best regards to Salnave and to Jean-Paul if he is in Paris and you see him." Bertin Salnave, the Haitian flute and saxophone player who had been in London in the SSO, recalled his association with Sidney Bechet and Roger Jean-Paul in a band at Rector's in London before 1922.[11] He also worked with Bechet and the ex-Orphanage trombonist Jacob Patrick, and then went to France and from there joined Arthur Briggs in Belgium, where they played at the Kursaal in Ostende with a banjo player named Alston Hughes from Trinidad.[12] Hughes may have been the husband of the Mrs. Hughes who knew of Harry Leekam's father dying. Jenkins had been sent a postcard of the Kursaal in September 1921, perhaps by one of his old SSO friends.

In September 1922 Edmund Jenkins was living in the "Europe" area of Paris, so named from its streets that bear the names of the cities of Europe. Jenkins lived at 44 rue de Moscou.[13]

Randall Lockhart's work in the summer of 1922 had been worthwhile, for he passed his examinations, and was called to the Bar on November 17, 1922.[14] He left England on December 31, 1922, and he wrote to Jenkins from Martinique on February 8, 1923, where his voyage had been terminated due to an epidemic of mild small pox in Dominica. He had not been able to get to Paris to see Jenkins, but he had kept in contact, and had heard that Jenkins

> had in mind within the next two years to return to the U.S.A., and that you would revert to your original plan. Why don't you think of the West Indies? You might be able to do something in a place like Trinidad, and you would have a freer life in the political sense than in the U.S.A.

Lockhart told Jenkins that he had heard that Harold Piper was very busy running his pharmaceutical business, which had money problems, and that "His ambition overleaps itself and that he has too many plans."

Lockhart was not the only old London friend to make contact with Edmund Jenkins in the winter of 1922–1923. He was also in touch with Herbert Henry of the QSH Syndicate Limited at the Queen's Hall in London.

CHAPTER 16

THE VERY BEST INSTRUMENTALIST OF ANY RACE

Herbert Henry wrote to "Dear Mr. Jenkins" on February 14, 1923:

> I have delayed answering your letter as I have been anticipating finding the time to run over to Paris when I should have given myself the pleasure of coming to see you. However, at the present time I am afraid that it cannot be managed for some time, so I am writing to ask you if there is a possibility of you rejoining the orchestra at the termination of your contract in Paris which, you tell me, occurs on 28th. inst. Reading between the lines of your letter, it seemed to me that you were implying that you might consider a change if the whole of your orchestra could be employed. Of course, I might have been wrong, but if that is the case I am afraid that it could not be managed as, quoting only one reason, there is now a strict law that no new dance orchestra can be imported unless the combination consists of 60% English subjects and 40% others. Perhaps you will be good enough to let me know your views. Please accept my cordial good wishes and kindest regards.

As African and Caribbean musicians would be subjects of the British Empire and thus "English," Henry was assuming that Edmund Jenkins's Paris band was French and American. It seems that Jenkins was acting as a band agent as well as a band leader, for he put the

Queen's Hall Roof band in touch with a Belgian impressario named Edmond Sayag.

Henry wrote—to "Dear Jenky"—on February 24, 1923, saying:

> The boys received your telegram, but as it was unsigned they thought that a practical joke was being played on them and immediately shewed it to me. I then told them who it was from and explained matters to them and they have asked me to negotiate on their behalf with M. Sayag. First of all, I must correct a statement I made re Thorburn's money. He started with me at £12 and he was such a good boy that I gave him an increase to £15, but I had forgotten that when I told you he was getting £12. Neither of them are over anxious to go to Paris, but they are willing to come for the same money as they are getting here—Thorburn £15.0.0. and Dixon £20.0.0. but they want to be paid in English money and a contract for two months.

The unstable French franc, which made France a cheap place to live, was one of the attractions of Paris in the 1920s for those people with private means. Henry continued:

> I can thoroughly recommend Thorburn who is one of the most reliable musicians I have ever had and is interested only in his work. M. Sayag will be pleased with him. I think that it is fortunate to get Dixon and and Thorburn together as they are friends and have worked together for months now, and know the same music and work in very much the same style as you and De Caillaux and should therefore fit in very well with the rest of the orchestra. Hoping to see you soon—sincerely yours.

Henry wrote a footnote on the typewritten letter: "Please ask M. Sayag to wire acceptance or otherwise." Pierre De Caillaux was a black American pianist who had composed *Turque* with Paul Wyer and had collaborated on other songs, including one with Jack Hylton recorded in 1922. Thorburn was probably Billy Thorburn, the pianist.

It seems likely that Jenkins and De Caillaux, working in Paris, exchanged with Dixon and Thorburn in London, for Jenkins was

playing at the Queen's Hall night club in early March 1923.
Edmund Jenkins was living at 28 Torrington Square, in the Bloomsbury area of London where he had been staying when Piper had
celebrated his return to Trinidad in December 1919. Getting back
to London after over a year away (except the rushed journey to
play at the Royal Academy of Music concert in July 1922) enabled
Jenkins to renew his contacts with his black and white London
friends, including Dr. Harry Leekam and his wife Mimi. The Iles
family, Alphonso Luke, Manyo Plange, John Alcindor, and John
Barbour-James had been involved in the recent visit to London of
King Sobhuza of Swaziland, when Barbour-James and Kwamina F.
Tandoh (King Amoah III) gave a concert in Acton on February 1,
1923.[1] King Sobhuza had come to London to inform the decision
makers that the blacks of Swaziland did not want to become part of
the Union of South Africa. During his visit Sobhuza stayed in
Maida Vale near John Alcindor.[2] He may have met Sol Plaatje,
who was back in London, still pleading the case for blacks in the
Union of South Africa.[3] Roland Hayes had been to France in early
1923, but was back in London giving a recital at the Wigmore Hall
on April 10.[4] From these friends Edmund Jenkins would have heard
of the death of Thomas McCants Stewart, which had been reported
in detail in the February 17 *West Africa*.

From 184 Sutherland Avenue, a street near Maida Vale which
crosses Lauderdale Road Babs Jones wrote to "Dear Mr. Jenkins"
on March 8, 1923, thanking him for a parcel containing a doll and a
bag, and adding "I expect you feel strange being back at "Queen's"
again, Daddy wasn't very surprised when I told him you were back
there!"[5]

Edmund Jenkins's return to London led to Mrs. Lily Lagois of 52
Hereford Road (near Alcindor's hospital in Paddington) writing on
April 13, 1923, "I've just heard of your return and am so delighted."
Her letter, which suggests that he took out a lease on an unfurnished
house and let Mrs. Lagois pay rent, from boarders, from that part
not used by herself, indicates that Jenkins had reasonable funds. She
also asked after an Edna Hatt, who seems to have been living in
Cornwall.

On April 25, 1923, a telegram arrived for Jenkins at 28 Torring-
ton Square: "IMPOSSIBLE VENIR LONDRES IMMEDIATEMENT LETTRE SUIT
GELLUSSEAU." The letter explaining why Gelluseau could not get to
London has not survived. Another telegram was sent from France

to Jenkins on April 25, 1923, which suggests that Jenkins had ordered an instrument, possibly a saxophone, from the Paris musical instrument manufacturer Selmer, and that one of his American friends in Paris was dealing with the matter: "SELMER IS SENDING INSTRUMENT BY HENRY ARNOLD LEAVING THURSDAY MORNING BEST WISHES THOMPSON." Thompson may be E. E. Thompson, the trumpet player who took over the SSO when Cook left and Jenkins refused Lattimore's offer, or Creighton Thompson, the musician who had been at the August 1921 Pan-African Congress in London.

In Paris Edmund Jenkins had kept in touch with the many black Americans visiting France, including Will Marion Cook. Cook wrote to Parson Jenkins from New York on March 7, 1923. His letter was on Clef Club stationery, 134 West 53rd Street, and was addressed to "Rev. Jenkins, Industrial School, Charleston, S.C." and read

> Dear Sir:—Want to congratulate you on your son Edmond [sic] T. Jenkins with whom I had a most wonderful association while in Paris. He is possibly the best Musician in the colored race; the very best instrumentalist in any race and one of the most perfect Gentlemen I have ever had the pleasure of meeting. I am making an extended tour of the United States with an Orchestra and Singers which I hope and think will be a great Financial success. I am hoping to persuade your son to come to America and join in this tour. I can make him adequate recompense and he himself can make a great American reputation. I am: respectfully yours—Will Marion Cook.

In London Jenkins and other blacks were treated rudely at a restaurant. He drafted a letter, amending it to make it curt. His deletions are shown below by slashes over his original words. Not all the writing is legible, especially where Jenkins completely crossed out words. Parts that have not been understood are indicated by dashes.

> ~~Dear~~ Sir,
> In justice to myself as a gentleman, albeit a man of colour, I wish to let you know ~~the class of people~~ who formed my party on Sunday last.

There were eight of us. Dr. and Mrs. Leekam and their brother from Trinidad and the Misses McDowell, daughters of ~~the Dr. McDowell of Chicago~~ an eminent Chicago physician. The party also included Mr. Lawrence Brown, ~~accompanist~~ student at the Royal College of Music and accompanist to Mr. Roland Hayes, the tenor. As for myself I am an Associate of the R. A. M. though now engaged in dance music, being Chef d'Orchestre of the Queens Hall Roof.

Having told these people that I had previously telephoned through and got permission to come on the Sunday night and having myself gone to the trouble of pointing out to the person who answered me over the phone (I was given to understand that it was Miss or Mrs. Mackenzie) ~~and I know which~~ that I was the *Saxophonist* of the Queens Hall Dance Orchestra /Jenkins by name; you will readily understand that as a cultured and refined gentleman, though a man of colour, some further expression was necessary on my part after your — — refusal to admit us. I want you to know the explanation I gave ~~I told them~~ because you must bear in mind that they are strangers to London and have not so extensive an — — idea of the various ~~classes~~ types of Englishmen as I have, seeing that I have been here ~~before since~~ a very long time.

I told them that you ~~after~~ — — were sufficiently ungentlemanly and contemptible to refer to my colour ~~and that~~ saying that it was against me, I — — apologised to them for having exposed them to possibly judging all Englishmen by the particular type you represented and I further informed them ~~that~~ in my eight years in London I have never been attacked in this manner before simply on account of the fact that when I go out I generally choose places of decidedly first class character such as the Criterion. — — Therefore I was not prepared for the kind of objection which could only come from a lower middle class establishment whose clientele no doubt is made up of a more or less ignorant, narrow minded and un travelled type.

I do not want you to think for a moment that any of the party, including myself, was annoyed or peeved over the matter, Our — — culture makes us aware of the difference of mentality in individuals concerning the point of colour.

Despite Edmund Jenkins's statement that none of the party was angry over the incident, his concern was over the reaction by Miss Minnie McDowell, for the others had been in Britain for years. His letter shows that he understood the class system of Britain.

Jenkins left Paris after his contract expired on February 28, and brought his car with him to London. He took it to the main Sunbeam-Talbot-Darracq depot in London's Acton, and various work was done to this sixteen horsepower car, registration XK 4352, including removal of a dent from the bonnet and repair of damage to the wings. This work may have been done after the farm gate incident that Dr. Leekam recalled years later. It cost forty-two pounds. He also went to the musical instrument repairer George Howarth at 73 York Street, Baker Street, and left his alto-saxophone and bass clarinet there for cleaning, regulating, and, for the saxophone, repadding. Jenkins paid a deposit of two pounds of May 8. Probably Thompson from Paris had arrived with the Selmer instrument and enabled Jenkins to hand his alto saxophone to Howarth for the repairs that the years of dance band work had made necessary.

Jenkins had been in London over two months when he hired an "omnibus and extra man" on May 19, 1923, from Thomas Wolfe's garage in Woburn Square, near his Torrington Square home, where his car was garaged. The hire of a bus and driver on Saturday May 19 by Jenkins may well have been for yet another of his American and Caribbean gatherings.

Edmund Jenkins had been in England for long enough to understand the game of cricket, and, from his Caribbean friends, learn of the fanatical devotion to this sport in the Caribbean. It was found in almost every area which had been in regular contact with Britain. Thomas H. Jackson, the Nigerian newspaper editor who had been in England and involved with the African Progress Union[6] and Sol Plaatje, had been a member of the Essex County Cricket Club.[7] Harry Leekam played cricket most summers and would have known of the 1922 visit to England of Major Harold Austin, who arranged for a team from the West Indies to tour England in the summer of 1923.[8] Austin returned to Barbados on the same ship as Randall Lockhart and arranged a team with five members from that island, five from Trinidad, three from British Guiana, and three from Jamaica.[9] The Jamaicans traveled to England on a different boat, arriving on April 26, 1923, according to Learie Constantine, who was one of the Trinidad group, who, with the others, arrived on April 27. Constantine's father had represented the West Indies in cricket matches in England before the war, and Constantine was to spend most of the rest of his life in England, playing cricket for English teams. In American sport black people were seldom seen, but England had several black sportsmen, including a black goal keeper for the northern soccer team of Preston North End during the late nineteenth century, James "Darkie" Peters who had represented England at rugby before World War I, and the cricketer Dr. C. H. Gunasekara from Ceylon who played for Harry Leekam's beloved Middlesex County cricket team in 1920.

The West Indies cricket team was playing at Cambridge on the day that Jenkins hired his bus, and he may have gone for the day to Cambridge with his Caribbean friends the Leekams, Alcindor, Luke, Harry and Nora Andrews, members of the Barbour-James and Iles families, and black Americans such as Hayes, Brown, the McDowells, and the Tucks. The week before the excursion Edmund Jenkins and Harry Leekam had produced another social event that gathered together blacks in London, but this time the guests included some of the leading black American entertainers working in London and the Caribbean cricketers.

CHAPTER 17

THE LEADER OF A
JAZZ-DANCE BAND

Leekam and Jenkins arranged the function in the name of the Coterie of Friends. Illustrious blacks gathered in honor of the West Indies cricket team in the Adelphi Rooms in the Paddington-Hyde Park area of London on the night of Sunday, May 13, 1923. The souvenir program described the Coterie as "dormant for the past twelve months or more (owing to the departure from London of some of its principal members) the Club can claim the credit of having given, during the period of its activity, social functions foremost in the Negro world of London." The master of ceremonies was Leyland Harper; the organizers were listed as Jenkins and Leekam; and the original members and founders of the Coterie were listed as Jenkins, Piper, Leekam, Lockhart, Luke, and McDougall. Years later Lockhart said McDougall may have married Rita Iles.[1]

The American guests listed in the program were Miss Florence Mills, Will Vodery, Shelton Brookes [sic], and "Mr. James P. Johnson and his Orchestra who have kindly taken charge of the Musical Programme." Will Vodery, who had been associated with Bert Williams until his death in 1922, had been in France with the U.S. forces in 1918. He and Will Marion Cook helped to develop the musical skills of Edward "Duke" Ellington, and Ellington—a regular employer of Jenkins Orphanage musicians—named some of his compositions after important black Americans. Bert Williams was one, and Willie "The Lion" Smith was another. He dedicated another composition to Florence Mills, who died in 1927 after an operation. His *Black Beauty* was one of the earliest of his compositions in this vein. Florence Mills was in London in 1923 working for the English theatrical impressario Charles B. Cochran, whose memoirs of a full and varied theatrical life in Britain and America have nothing but praise for her. She was an impressive performer and her early death was a great loss to American entertainment. It was felt deeply in the black community, and was to be commented on by Sol Plaatje, who had first met Miss Mills in New York in 1921 when she was appearing in the all-black show *Shuffle Along*, which had been produced by Noble Sissle (a sergeant with Lt. Mikell in James Europe's 369 Regiment band in France), Eubie Blake, Aubrey Lyles, and Flournoy Miller.

Plaatje wrote in South Africa of Florence Mills in London in May 1923.

> I next met her at Piccadilly Pavilion where she was starred in "Dover Street to Dixie" a partly coloured production, at £260 per week. Her lucky husband was also in the cast. By permission of Mr. Cochran, the London Theatre King, three members of the troupe sang gratuitously at my farewell concert on my last Sunday in London before I sailed for the Cape. The London promoters considered their action extremely generous having regard to the standing fee of £77 paid to their band when engaged to play at a ball any night after the close of their Piccadilly performance.[2]

Jenkins and Leekam must have paid that amount in order to hire the orchestra of James P. "Jimmie" Johnson, although Johnson was working for another black show in London—the *Plantation Days Company* at the Empire Theater in Leicester Square.[3]

The orchestra for *Dover Street to Dixie* was led by Will Vodery with song writer Shelton Brooks. Brooks was well known through his very popular songs *Darktown Strutters' Ball* and *Some of These Days*. Florence Mills's husband was Ulysses "Slow Kid" Thompson, a greatly experienced tap dancer and entertainer who had traveled with medicine shows in the South, taught whites in New York to dance the Castle way, and had worked in *Shuffle Along*.[4] Vodery had worked with Will Marion Cook, Dunbar, Hogan,

Cole, and others,[5] as well as with Brooks in New York in July 1922.[6]

Johnson was a little older than Edmund Jenkins, and greatly experienced. He had been working in the New York area for years, associating with Willie "The Lion" Smith and becoming Thomas "Fats" Waller's teacher. He influenced Ellington, but his innovative piano style received less public notice than that of his extrovert pupil Waller. Johnson had cut piano rolls in New York in 1921, including his own composition *Carolina Shout*, still a test piece for jazz pianists.

The success of *Shuffle Along* in New York in 1921 was outstanding, and the show toured America after it ended its long run. Other all-black shows followed, but by 1923 the novelty had worn off.[7] Those blacks who had visited Europe in the armed forces, in the various dance groups such as Haston's and Dan Kildaire's, and former Southern Syncopated Orchestra musicians such as Bechet, Robert Young, and Briggs, told their friends of the welcome that black Americans would receive in Europe, of the lack of Jim Crow, and the booming dance world. Black Americans took advantage of European show business being some years behind that of the United States, and followed the path that had been marked by Frank Johnson, the Fisk Singers, James Bland, and Arabella Fields.

Britain welcomed *Dover Street to Dixie. Dancing World* said:

> There are still large numbers of people who think that jazz is dead, or dying, or about to die. This illusion has persisted now for two or three years, and whenever any musical novelty makes its appearance in our ballrooms, one is sure to read that jazz, as a logical consequence, is about to shuffle off its mortal coil. In "Dover Street To Dixie", however, it is still shufflin' along, brilliantly assisted by Will Vodery.[8]

This monthly magazine reviewed the show, saying that "it brims over with talent"[9] and commented on the black half of the show, which was entitled *Plantation Review* or *Revue*, that it "proves conclusively that white people are not the only ones who can sing and dance, despite the abusive nonsense which is still talked on the subject."[10] It also mentions the singing of Florence Mills and Edith

Wilson and the possible problems with Ministry of Labour work permits.

Edmund Jenkins would surely have seen this show in London, and he certainly got to know Will Vodery at this time. He knew Minnie McDowell—one of the irons in the fire, as Lockhart might have commented—and introduced her to his London friends Lawrence Brown, the Leekams, Tony and Jeanette Tuck, and probably others. Minnie left England on the White Star Line's *Majestic,* and her note, just dated "Sunday" says

> Dearest Teddy
>
> Received both your wonderful wires and you don't know how much they meant to me. I only wish I could turn right around and come back to London. We have had a wonderful trip. . . . Enjoy the company of Sheba but don't fall in *love. Love* me and me only, will you darling? The weather has been wonderful and the trip most pleasing. Ans at once and send mail to 158 W 131st c/o Sumer New York. I shall stay there until I hear from you and then I shall wire home for money and go to good old Chi. Best regards to the Tucks and Mr. Brown. With much love I remain as ever—yours Minnie.

Tony Tuck of The Versatile Three was living at 1 Doughty Street, on the southern edge of Bloomsbury. It was to Jenkins, care of Tuck, that Edmond Sayag, the director of the Kursaal in Ostende, Belgium, sent a letter dated June 16, 1923, regarding some event at the concert hall on July 7, 1923. Edmund Jenkins had given Tuck's address to Sayag, and Henry "Harry" Gordon Andrews's business address to Will Marion Cook. Harry and Nora Andrews lived in Castellain Mansions, around the corner from Jenkins's 1921 home at Lauderdale Mansions in the Maida Vale district where so many of Jenkins's friends lived.

Harry and Nora Andrews had established their West Indies merchants, planters, and shippers business in November 1921, with Harry in partnership with Albert Logette, a translator. Logette left in May 1922, perhaps the cause or the result of the financial troubles Lockhart had written about to Jenkins.[11] The firm—Gordon Andrews and Company, Holborn, London—received a letter from

New York addressed to "Mr. J. Edmunds Jenkins." It was from C. A. Parker of G. Lewis Theatrical Enterprises of New York and was dated June 1, 1923.

> With reference to a cablegram which you received from Will Marion Cook. For a number of years I have been engaged in the music business in Ohio. I came to New York in February and for the past few weeks have been associated with Mr. Cook in some of his activities. On the 20th of May he gave a concert at the Century Theatre which was reputed to be the most artistic concert ever given in New York. From this success, Mr. Cook was given the impression to put on a colored revue. There is not a colored show on Broadway to-day and the time is ripe to do BIG things.
>
> Mr. Cook realizes that in asking you to come here and assist him would be at a sacrifice to you, but feels that the Broadway opportunity will more than make up the difference. In addition to the revue, it would be possible for you to have another engagement after the show. He has authorized me to offer you $125 per week in view of the above mentioned facts and feels that you should do a great deal more than this.
>
> Mr. Lars Moen is putting on a show which he claims will surpass "Ziegfeld's Follies," and Mr. Cook has recommended you. You should receive a letter from Mr. Moen about same. Mr. Cook has asked me to say that Jimmie Johnson has spoken very highly of the kind treatment which you showed him and you can rest assured that both of them appreciated it very much. Please consider the above proposition very carefully and realize that this will be the beginning of some very large activities in the entertaining line.
>
> There is a wonderful chance for a colored Symphony and the men who are backing Cook are eager to help all they can to promote same and make it international in scope. Mr. Cook needs your assistance in training etc and we hope you will give us an affirmative answer at once. Such people as Gilpin, Abbie Mitchell, Richard Harrison, Alberta Hunter and others will make this the sensation of New York.
>
> Hoping to hear from you by return mail . . .

Parker added his own address, 263 W 139th Street, and, from other evidence, it seems that Edmund Jenkins accepted this offer.

Edmund Jenkins was still earning substantial amounts, and Parker's offer was not much more than that paid to Dixon by Henry, so Jenkins's plans to return to the United States, which Lockhart had known about before he left England, may have been after he had acquired a reasonable amount of capital. He was able to lend James O'Farrell Fletcher, a Trinidad medical man of 1b, Chapel Street, London NW1, thirty pounds on July 6, 1923.[12] Jenkins's bank account in Paris was in the French associates of his London bank, and their statement for the first six months of 1923 has survived. Jenkins's address is 44 rue de Moscou. On January 1, 1923, he had francs 20,081.60 (about £300, or $1,400). He deposited fr7,000 on January 19, fr2,500 on January 29, and fr4,000 on February 15, 1923. If these were his earnings, he had fr2,500 in ten days ($170), which compares to Parker's offer of $125 for a week. Living costs were probably lower in Paris and London than in New York. The statement shows two checks paid—one on March 3 for fr1,000, and a second on May 7 for fr1,395. The former is probably the cash withdrawn for his trip to rejoin Henry at the Queen's Hall, and the latter a third-party check and not evidence that Jenkins was back in Paris before the Coterie cricket team entertainment of May 13.

Edmund Jenkins may have been back in France, or in Belgium, for the July 7, 1923, event at the Kursaal. First, the "season" in London resulted in the theaters closing in the summer, and, second, Sayag wrote to Jenkins at 26 rue Pasquier, Paris, from Ostende on August 29, 1923. This concerned a job at the Club Daunou in Paris, for a band of six pieces to play from five to seven o'clock for fr350. Jenkins would be free to play elsewhere in the evening, wrote Sayag. Bertin Salnave recalled "I played with him at the Daunou in Paris under the leadership of Monsieur Ritouc. It was there that he began to play his flashy variations."[13] The Club Daunou was at 7, rue Daunou, opposite Ciro's Club, about fifteen minutes from Jenkins's rue de Moscou home, and less from the rue Pasquier. Jenkins had played there before August 1923, for a postcard addressed "E Jenkins Club Daunou Paris" from Monte Carlo has survived the years. Dated by hand December 12, it was probably mailed in December 1922. The handwriting and the odd use of "business" where "job" would be more natural indicate the writer was a white Western European. "I think this kind of climate would suit you better than Paris. You should try to get a business here next winter. My best regards to M. de Caillaux. . . ."

A postcard, from three girls Magdeleine Solas, Marguerite Hefti, and "Cloche," was mailed but the postmark is unreadable. Addressed to "Monsieur Edmund T. Jenkins, 26 rue Pasquier, Paris," it has pencil calculations in Jenkins's hand on it—"238 × 5 = 1190" —which appears to be a band calculation.

On September 12, 1923, one of Jenkins's friends, "Peggy," writing from 84 Tavistock Crescent in, according to the writer, London's Notting Hill district, but actually nearer to Alcindor's hospital and the Maida Vale district where so many of Jenkins's London friends lived, replied to Jenkins's postcard received that morning. "Now, re the week end, it's really awfully sweet of you to suggest my coming to Ostende, but when I 'look around' as it were, I seem effaced with so many difficulties. . . . " Peggy asked Jenkins "Have you decided to stay on the Continent, then? Perhaps I shall see you when you come to London, shall I?"

In late September 1923 Edmund Jenkins was back in London. He wrote but did not mail a postcard to Tonia Kato of 18, Morshead Mansion, Maida Vale, just a few yards from Lauderdale Mansions. Jenkins's links with the Kato family seem to have been quite close, for he kept a Christmas card they mailed to him. His card was headed 26 rue Pasquier October 18, 1923: "Left without seeing you but shall be back in London next month, and shall stay until the end of November before sailing to New York, so shall hope to see you all again. As ever, with love to all—Teddy."[14]

Jenkins had been in London at the Queen's Hall from March until July; in Paris in July and perhaps Belgium, too; in Paris in August; and in Belgium in September, before getting back to London at the end of September. He wrote a long letter to his stepmother Mrs. Eloise C. Jenkins from Ostende on September 6, 1923:

My Dear little step mother

What a disgraceful son you have to have utterly suspended correspondence so indefinitely! The last year has been one of much thought for me and I seem to have been busy every moment thinking what was the best thing for me to do. This along with the fact that I have had practical difficulties in the way of contending with problems which continually faced me in my daily work left me with very little time for the pleasure and repose I would receive from the methodical correspondence I revelled in in the earlier days of my youth. I did not set out to make such a high sounding and pedantic sentence as the last one proves to be but it certainly explains how I have kept procrastinating in the matter of writing. At first when I went to Paris last year I did not know whether to stay there or return to London. After that I had another offer in London[15] and I was not sure whether I should take that or whether I should stay in Paris; finally after a lot of worrying as to what I should do I suddenly returned to London for three months during which time I worried myself thinking whether I should accept an offer in Belgium and again in Paris.[16] In the meantime I had received an offer from New York from a somewhat dubious albeit well meaning source.[17] All these things so clouded my mind that along with my daily work I did not find time and repose for correspondence as I have explained above.

Jenkins had received a letter from Edwin Harleston, the painter relative of his stepmother, asking for special paints: "His letter reached me about a couple of months after it had been written and being in London at the time I could not get the pastels."

Edmund Jenkins had written to Charleston, telling them of Minnie McDowell from Chicago:

I am rather curious to know how you all took the news I sent you in my letter to Paps in the Spring from London telling him that I was thinking of being engaged to a girl from Chicago. A friend of mine, a distinguished musician from New York, kept me from making such a foolish step.[18] I am greatly indebted to him for keeping me from making an almost irrevocably compromising step. He knew the girl better than I did and showed me wherein I would be making a grave mistake. Subsequent happenings proved him to be absolutely correct. So no doubt when you see me again I shall still be single, unmarried and dis-engaged.

7. Mrs. Eloise C. Harleston Jenkins, Charleston, S.C.,
1924. Original photograph taken by Edmund Jenkins.
*From a negative in the possession of the late Edwina
Fleming of Charleston, S.C.*

Jenkins's letter explained his plans "After the 16th inst I am planning to go to London for about a week and after that I shall return to Paris where I shall be until the end of October when I hope to take a boat for New York—to spend Xmas at home." He gave his Paris address as 26 rue Pasquier, and "in London mail will reach me at 1 Doughty Street, W.C. c/o Tuck."

Edmund Jenkins was sent a postcard from Digoin, a small town on the upper reaches of the Loire near Lyon. Postmarked September 12, 1923, it was addressed to "Monsieur Jenkins, Chef d'Orchestre Jazz-Band, Kursaal, Ostende, Belgique." The writer said that he would be returning to Paris, asked if Jenkins would be going there, if the Daunou would open without us "sans nous," and gave greetings to "Mister Holmes." Nine years after entering the Royal Academy of Music Edmund Jenkins was the leader of a jazz-dance band at the resort town of Ostende on the coast of Belgium, apparently no nearer the ambitions he had discussed with Piper and Lockhart four and more years before in London.

CHAPTER 18

A CONCERT FOR AFRICA

Edmund Jenkins was not forgotten in America. The letterhead stationery used by the Jenkins Orphanage, which shows that there were five bands and two concert choirs of one hundred voices each "that go out each summer when the school closes to raise funds for the institution. They are invited to all portions of the country, in Europe as well, when transportation is sent in advance," includes "Prof. E. T. Jenkins" in the list of Orphan Aid Society Board members.[1] From Blanche H. Vashon of Sumner High School in Saint Louis, Missouri, Jenkins received a letter dated October 24, 1923, despite its being addressed to him at the Royal College of Music, London. This young student told Jenkins that her English teacher Robert P. Hatts "was teaching at the Atlanta Baptist College in Atlanta, Georgia, in 1910, at the same time you were a pupil there. . . . Having had many experiences which would be of the deepest interest to us, I hope you will impart some of them, that we here at Sumner High might know and profit by them." No doubt Hatts had been reminded of Jenkins from Brawley's writings.

Jenkins's plan to leave France in October was changed, and he was to spend much of November 1923 in London. At the beginning of November the annual meeting of the African Progress Union took place at the Denison House, Victoria, offices of John Harris's antislavery group. Dr. John Alcindor spoke to about thirty people, and explained that "Mr. E. T. Jenkins, ARAM, a member of the committee, was away in Paris just now."[2] Others at the small gathering on November 6 were John Harris, the treasurer John Barbour-James, and Dr. W. E. B. Du Bois, who gave details of his plans for the Pan-African Congress that was to be held in the same building on November 7 and 8. Alcindor was concerned about the actions of white settlers in east Africa, who were endeavoring to make the Africans work for them, and remarked "that the conditions under which the natives worked in Kenya were tantamount to slavery."[3] He was reelected head of the APU for two years.

The Pan-African Congress was badly planned, and led to critical comments in *West Africa* and *The African World.* The latter commented on November 17, 1923, "Want of acquaintance with the conditions of life in British West Africa seemed rather to distinguish the speakers at the Pan-African Congress, and it is a little difficult to discover upon what common ground the representatives of the American negroes and those of Sierra Leone, the Gold Coast, and Nigeria can meet. But that is not to cast any word of deprecation on the value of this Congress and its enlightening tendencies."[4]

The visiting Americans mixed with the APU's Dr. and Mrs. Alcindor, and Barbour-James, visiting the site of the West Africa pavilion at Wembley on November 9 with Lady Guggisberg,[5] who had been an actress before she married Gordon Guggisberg. They had been in the Gold Coast before World War I, and Guggisberg, a friend of Barbour-James,[6] was now governor of the Gold Coast and a supporter of Aggrey. Barbour-James's friend Kwamina F. Tandoh (King Amoah III) had been at the Pan-African Congress, and from these friends Edmund Jenkins made contact with the Americans.

George Lattimore had been helping Sol Plaatje, who had left England in mid-October, after the party with three members of the cast of *Dover Street to Dixie,* and a concert in the Mortimer Hall, Mortimer Street, London, on October 9, 1923, which included Evelyn Dove, Mrs. Drysdale, the Caribbean soprano Mary Lawrence, and Miss Coleridge-Taylor.[7] Lattimore was in contact with Jenkins, who may have arrived in London in time to renew his contacts with Du Bois. Jenkins drafted a letter:

Dear Mr. Lattimore,

I arrived safely in Paris without any untoward incident, apart from the uncomfortable fact that I had to ride all the way from Calais to Paris in the corridor. Never will be caught like

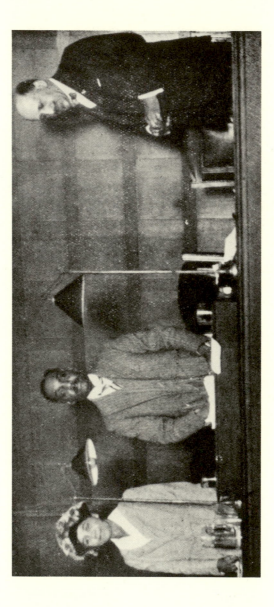

8. Dr. John Alcindor and Dr. W. E. B. Du Bois at the Pan-African Congress, London, 1923. *From West Africa, November 17, 1923, p. 1394. Copyright The British Library.*

that again while its possible to reserve seats in advance. With reference to our chat at the station and the proposition you have in mind re symphony concert I must say that I am deeply interested. I have thought that inasmuch as I have decided to go home for Xmas ~~I must suggest to you that before I~~ —— it would perhaps be wise for you to judge the temper of the multitude by giving an orchestral concert of Negro music between now and the 1st of December.

The letter is sketched in haste, and not all words are clear. Jenkins suggested that Dvořák's *New World Symphony* and Coleridge-Taylor's *Variations on an African Air*, with, "perhaps, my own 'Folk Rhapsody' " would be the program. "To present properly the above mentioned three works it would necessitate an orchestra of —— forty musicians. With first class musicians I could do the concert with two rehearsals, one to take place a week before it," the other to be on the morning of the concert. "Perhaps also this concert could be arranged on a date so as to —— til the delegates on their way back from Lisbon. I write in haste to put this suggestion before you as whatever is done about it will be done at once."

Jenkins listed the forty-two instruments required and reduced the four horns to two in a calculation on the single sheet of paper he had used for the draft. The delegates Jenkins mentioned were the Americans of the Pan-African Congress, which had been scheduled to meet in Lisbon, Portugal, in August 1923, but went there in late November from London. Du Bois sailed from Lisbon to Africa, making his first visit to the continent. The confusion in reports on Du Bois and the Pan-African Congresses of 1919, 1921, and 1923 is partly due to the lack of programs, reports, and minutes, and partly due to the unbusinesslike way that Du Bois arranged everything.[8] Jenkins's conversation with Lattimore at London's Victoria Station, where he took the Paris train, may have been after the last session of the Congress at the nearby Denison House, where the American delegates would have avoided showing their strained relations with the Portuguese *Liga Africana* and the confusion of the meetings, leaving Jenkins and Lattimore to assume that the Lisbon gathering would be within four or five days of November 8, 1923.

Jenkins was in London in late November, and went to see his

bank manager at 14 Shepherd's Bush Green, which was yards from the White City exhibition ground where he had played with his father's band years before. The bank manager wrote to him at 1 Doughty Street on November 30, "I regret that I cannot see my way to make any advance, therefore, any cheque drawn must be provided for in *sterling*." Jenkins was probably having difficulty getting his francs from Paris.

Jenkins arranged to have his Talbot Darracq motor car with him in the United States, and so paid £17-11-0 (£17.55, or $80) on December 3, 1923, to enable it to be shipped to New York on the *Maryland*.[9] He was in Charleston for Christmas 1923, and he worked on a serious composition.

CHAPTER 19

A MUSIC SCHOOL, PUBLISHING FIRM, AND ORCHESTRA

The United States in late 1923 was quite different from the country Jenkins left in 1914 and from the America he had traveled through in August-September 1920. The boll weevil had destroyed the cotton crop, moving slowly from Mexico through the southern states, reaching South Carolina in the early 1920s. Black laborers and their families left the destroyed countryside, pushed by the racism of the whites and the poverty of their existence as agricultural workers and pulled by the glowing reports of economic and social opportunity in the North. The expansion of the North's industries during the war, combined with the disruption in the flow of the hundreds of thousands of European immigrants, had started blacks moving North. Ill-educated, superstitious, and rustic, they were forced to live in ghettoes, in overcrowded apartments soon turned into slums by neglect. Marcus Garvey's UNIA had given them pride in their color, and held out a beacon of hope in economic self-sufficiency through a black-owned shipping line and other businesses, and in the Zionist-like promise of "back to Africa." Over half a million dollars were poured into these activities and squandered through petty corruption and mismanagement. Garvey's promises, parades, and uniforms made ghetto life bearable.

Other blacks disliked Garvey—an upstart Jamaican who had gained leadership of hundreds of thousands of blacks in America. Other black leaders such as A. Philip Randolph advocated socialism in his magazine *The Messenger;* in 1923 the Urban League, believing in self-help and uplift, started its monthly magazine *Opportunity* and continued with its efforts to reduce ill health and tuberculosis in black ghettoes. The NAACP's *The Crisis* presented America's race problems to an international audience, and was the work of Du Bois and Jessie Fauset.

The entertainment industry had changed, for sales of recordings were four times their 1914 level, and, in 1920, it had been encouraged to produce black popular music and black art songs on disc.[1] In 1921 Harry Pace and W. C. Handy had established a black recording company called Black Swan; in Chicago in March 1923 the first of a series of regular recordings by a black band were made by Joe "King" Oliver, with twenty-two year-old Louis Armstrong on second cornet. In 1923 in New York Bessie Smith recorded *Down Hearted Blues*, a song that had already been recorded by Alberta Hunter, but Smith's was to sell 258,000 copies in 1923.[2]

Edmund Jenkins's American contacts in Britain had been busy in America: Bessie Smith appeared with Bechet in a New York show entitled *How Come?;*[3] Shelton Brooks had recorded for Okeh in April;[4] and the orphanage pupils Gus "Rice" Aitken (or Aiken) and Eugene "Bud" Aitken recorded with Perry Bradford in May and August 1923. Bradford had been responsible for the 1920 recording of *Crazy Blues* that had started the regular recording of black musicians. Gus Aitken's opportunity had come when Bradford's regular trumpeter Johnny Dunn left him to work in London with *Dover Street to Dixie.*

The illegal drinking and gambling clubs run in the big cities offered black jazz musicians and entertainers many opportunities to appear before a white audience; the increased wealth in the black community and the overcrowded living conditions encouraged blacks to seek diversion at both illegal and legal entertainment spots. The weekly black paper of Chicago, *The Defender,* was full of "race" news, and it was distributed through the South by the Pullman car porters, usually black southerners. The most populated black area in the world was Harlem, in New York City, where many quasi-religious and political cults other than Garvey's had their headquarters. Three hundred thousand dollars were spent on the 138th Street Abyssinian Baptist Church, whose minister, Adam Clayton Powell, Sr., was a friend of Parson Jenkins.[5]

In the summer of 1923 the first racially mixed recordings in the

United States were made when the New Orleans pianist Ferd "Jelly Roll" Morton recorded with the white New Orleans Rhythm Kings for the Gennett label.[6] In June 1923 Fisk-University-educated Flournoy Miller and Aubrey Lyles started work on a new black show entitled Runnin' Wild[7], which was to feature James P. Johnson's songs *Runnin' Wild* and *Charleston.* It was the only successful black show to open in New York until September 1924.[8]

In January 1924 the New York *Age* advertised one of Will Marion Cook's presentations, Negro Nuances, which was to begin at the Times Square Theater on Sunday, January 27, 1924. Cook's wife Abbie Mitchell, Gertrude Saunders (who later "stole" Bessie Smith's husband), "the Misses Hughes, Welch, Duncan, and Harvey, who compose the ladies' quartet of Runnin' Wild," Paul Robeson, Alberta Hunter, and Edith Wilson were listed. Robeson had been in London in 1923 appearing in *Taboo*; Edith Wilson had been in *Dover Street to Dixie* in London in May 1923; Georgia Harvey had recorded for Black Swan. Cook's concert also included an "orchestra of twenty-five, under the direction of Edward [*sic*] T. Jenkins of London and Will Marion Cook, the Old Master, will render Negro spirituals, jazz music, modern Negro classics and part songs as only Negroes can. The quintessence of jazz." Tickets were priced from $1.00 to $3.50.

The day before the concert the *Age* carried another announcement, with Jenkins's first name corrected, stating that the "Negro Musical Night" had been moved to the 44th Street Theater. Cook had misjudged public feeling, and his show was a failure. Edmund Jenkins wrote to his father from Baltimore, Maryland, on February 1, 1924, "The Cook concert was not at all a success and I was lucky in being able to get out of having anything to do with the program just at the last moment." Edmund Jenkins was staying with Robert "Bob" Young at 501 Sandford Place; Young had been with Bechet and Briggs at the Buckingham Palace staff garden party in August 1919. Edmund Jenkins had been busy in his few weeks in America, for his letter continued:

> Since coming to New York I have discussed the music publishing business idea with a gentleman who knows the business from A to Z seeing that he has been in some way connected with that kind of business all of his life, and has started as

stock boy on up to arranger and advising editor to first class
Chicago and New York publishing houses. He has an office of
his own on Broadway where he specialises in arranging the
music of such famous productions as Ziegfeld Follies etc. He
told me how it was that the other colored publishing company came to give up business. And ended up volunteering to
go into business with me. By the way, I must tell you that his
name is W. H. Vodery. I met him in London and it is at his
flat I have been staying in New York.

Edmund Jenkins explained to his father that "the idea came to me
when I was in Charleston," and that Vodery knew "every angle of
the business and with his reputation in the lighter and popular
theatrical music and with my reputation as an exponent of the
classic and artistic composition we ought to make a real big concern all of this added with the business sagacity of my friend Mr.
Robert Young, whom I hope to interest more in the publishing
line." The three of them were to discuss the plan in New York "in a
few days," and Edmund wanted his father to back him with one to
two thousand dollars.

Edmund's work in Charleston that Christmas appears to have
been on a new folk rhapsody, and he told his father "I think I am
well on my way to have my rhapsody performed, having been
promised letters of introduction to the symphony orchestra conductor by the music critic of the New York Herald. I am to call on
him upon my return to New York."

His associations with white musicians in England and France had
not prepared him for the race restrictions of U.S. concert halls. By
April 1924 he was less buoyant—the scheme to cooperate with
Robert Young and Will Vodery came to nothing; by the time he
wrote to his stepmother from 232 West 138th Street, where he was
staying with someone named Spiller, he had "decided that New
York is the only place to pull off the big ideas I have and I am trying
to get settled here." He asked for the New York addresses of T. L.
Grant and other friends of the orphanage. His car was still in storage—as soon as he could get it out of storage and have a "fairly
permanent residence" settled, he planned to discuss matters with
his father in Charleston. He had been working in Baltimore, but

had "given up completely the Baltimore idea as being impracticable to attain the big things I want to do."

Edmund Jenkins had misjudged America. Gwendolyn Bennett of *Opportunity* met him in the winter of 1923–1924 and later wrote: "He was filled with enthusiasm about some sort of musical plan that he had come to America with the hope of seeing realised. I saw him again in the Fall of 1924, after about a year's disillusionment. It seems that having lived abroad for so long a time he had forgotten the frightful prejudice that hounds the American Negro's every thought and action."[9] Bennett added that "the Jenkins that I saw as he was about to leave for Paris was a far different man from the idealist that I had met the winter before."

Edmund Jenkins had broken away from Cook's *Negro Nuances* which was later to involve over twenty minutes of music by Sidney Bechet and James P. Johnson.[10] He had traveled to Chicago, where the *Defender* noted his visit to their office in July. He visited Brawley and "talked far into the night—of his dreams of a great school of music, of a publishing firm, of an orchestra that should tour the country. Something spurred him on to one great effort. He tried Washington, and Baltimore, and New York."[11]

Jenkins told Bennett that "the self-centeredness, passive resistance and artificial sincerity combined with the utter lack of cooperation among those who are described as the leaders in Negro artistic progress clearly demonstrated to me how futile my plans were for immediate consideration, unless I had a fortune with which to launch my ideals and ideas." His ideals were a black symphony orchestra, a black school of music, a music publishing company, and a central institution for black music "and all that pertains thereto."[12] Jenkins appears to have written from Europe to Bennett: "I found that in America the dollar talks and no one is found wanting in rallying to its stentorian tones whatever may be his or her professed ideals." Brawley wrote that "at best he received only a dubious smile. At last he wrote to say that all was of no avail and that he was going back to Paris."[13]

Edmund Jenkins was in America during the "Harlem Renaissance," when the black cultural achievement in literature, poetry, and painting, was accepted by critics, became popular with the artistic elite, and patronized by white and black alike. The black artistic leaders who had failed to support Jenkins's schemes were heading toward a cultural maturity that had almost come to terms with black America. The problem of such blacks was similar to that of Mrs. Thurber when she had tried to encourage Dvořák to produce a truly American piece of music, for white Americans had difficulty in coming to terms with their identity. They had given up a European identity and had found another, but without folk roots and heritage.

Alain Leroy Locke, a brilliant black scholar who had studied in England as a Rhodes Scholar from 1907, was the leader in the Harlem Renaissance, encouraging artistic self-consciousness and awareness of black achievement and past cultural activities. Just as Marcus Garvey had insisted that blacks should be aware of their cultural past and should cease to be brown copies of white America (he encouraged black dolls for babies and did not accept the skin-lightening cream and hair-straightener advertisements found in most black publications), Locke tried to end the alienation of the black intellectual. Locke's *The New Negro: An Interpretation* was published in New York in 1925. He encouraged every black talent and got to know Edmund Jenkins, whom he followed to Europe in 1925.

Jenkins's sister Mildred was attending Hartshorn Memorial College in Richmond, Virginia, with Olive Harleston, who had left Wigan in 1920 after her education had ended in England. Edmund Jenkins called at this all-girls' school in September 1924, and gave a short piano recital. He discussed his future plans with his sister and half-sister. In 1979 Olive advised John Chilton that she remembered Edmund saying that he had thought his future was in Europe.

In the summer of 1924 Edmund Jenkins applied for a new passport, describing his profession as "composer and conductor." He planned to leave New York on the *Paris* on October 1, 1924. His months in America made him readjust his spelling, for his complexion was now "colored." He gave his address as care of Des Verney, 150 West 130th Street in New York City. This was to cause him considerable anxiety, for his new passport did not reach him (Des Verney's address was 150 West 131st Street), and, on the day before the *Paris* was due to sail, he applied for a duplicate passport.[14]

One year later Des Verney's apartment would be the site at

which A. Philip Randolph, the black socialist and publisher of *The Messenger*; William Des Verney, an official of the Pullman Company staff association; Ashley L. Totten; and Roy Lancaster agreed to organize the U.S. black sleeping car porters.[15] The meeting in 1925 was to lead to the first successful black trade union in America, the Brotherhood of Sleeping Car Porters. William Des Verney is thought to have been a relative of Jenkins.[16] Even if Edmund Jenkins did not know his address, he knew him well enough to leave his car with him to sell.

CHAPTER 20

"I WILL GET THIS CHANCE IN EUROPE"

Edmund Jenkins returned to Paris, where he found a home (an apartment or rooms) at 27 rue Lécluse, in the same Europe area of Paris but a little further north than rue de Moscou. On October 24, 1924, he wrote to his father, saying that he was to start work on November 1. "I am also engaged on the libretto for a musical play, a kind of operetta which I hope to get presented at a Paris theatre when I get through writing the music for it. I shall commence on the music as soon as I get my libretto translated into French. An influential and rich man has intimated to me that if in his opinion the play is a good one he will produce it for me."

Edmund hoped that it would be a success as it would enable him "to have you come over here and see it." His hopes were not realized. By March 1925 Edmund Jenkins was directing a band of black musicians in Paris, called The International Seven. Their planned visit to Italy, to play before the king of Italy at the beginning of March 1925 was publicized in the Chicago *Defender* of April 4, 1925, which listed the other members of the group, all expatriate black Americans like Jenkins.[1]

He kept in touch with developments in black music in America. In 1924 exorphanage musician Tom Delaney's *Nobody Knows the Way I Feel Dis Mornin'* was recorded for Gennett by a group that included Bechet and Alberta Hunter. The trumpet player was Louis Armstrong. Another Charleston black, Chris Smith, had written *Ballin' the Jack*, which was very successful in 1913, and had led a band that had included the father of Charleston-born Thaddeus Drayton. Thaddeus Drayton was later to comment on the hit dance of the mid-1920s, James P. Johnson's *Charleston*, which had first appeared in *Runnin' Wild* in October 1923 at New York's Colonial Theater,[2] saying that he had seen it in Charleston in 1903.[3] Noble Sissle claimed that he knew it in Savannah about 1905.[4] By 1925 it was a world sensation. It spread faster than the Castle-Europe fox trot and became the symbol of the age. Chris Smith's *Cake Walking Babies from Home* was also recorded by Hunter, Bechet, and Armstrong that session.

Paramount had taken over the Black Swan label, and, by the middle of 1924, their catalog included the "Negro National Anthem" *Lift Every Voice and Sing*, which had been written by the Johnson brothers; "Hattie King Reavis of Will Marion Cook's English Syncopated Orchestra" singing *There Is a Green Hill Far Away*, and recordings by Kemper Harreld, Ethel Waters, and Maud de Forrest.[5] The Aitken brothers recorded Shelton Brooks's *Here's Your Opportunity.*[6]

Florence Mills was appearing in Cochran's *Dixie to Broadway* in New York, with the band directed by Will Vodery.[7] Josephine Baker, who had worked with *Shuffle Along*, opened at the Colonial Theater in New York in *Chocolate Dandies* in September 1924 and later moved to Paris. In the 1920s Paris was probably second only to Berlin as a cosmopolitan, artistic, and culturally daring city. Black performers, the exotic, the unconventional—all were in vogue.

Edmund Jenkins's musical play was an operatic revue, which his potential backer found too expensive to support, according to a letter Jenkins wrote to his father from rue Lécluse on February 3, 1925. The visit to Charleston had been an influence on this work, which included scenes set in the cotton fields, among the palmetto and pine trees of Carolina, and a fight scene between smugglers and revenue officers, which may be due to the gin-running of Prohibition America.[8]

But the plans he had hoped to see come to some fruition in America were not abandoned, for his letter to Parson Jenkins continued:

> I have a wonderful opportunity of going into the music publishing business on my own in a kind of small way to begin

with, but unfortunately I lack at present the necessary capital to set myself up in an office. That is all I need to start with, just a real decent office in the proper district, and I would have the field practically to myself in the way of arranging French tunes in the popular American fashion. If I can get this office going and then get my play produced I would be in a position to make a fortune as I would then publish the music of the play myself and thereby obtain all of the profit instead of a mere ten or twenty per cent which the publishers give composers.

He asked his father if he could contract a loan of three thousand dollars repayable over two years, which would be repaid by Edmund "long before that time." "I cannot do it over here because I have no property against which loaning organisations would make me any advance. If you could possibly get some firm in Charleston or in any part of the states to make those arrangements for me I assure you you will have given me the lift I need just now to get in the way of making some really big money."

Edmund Jenkins was certain of the success of the plan, provided he was not rushed into repaying the loan, and he assured his father that he would continue working "until the work at the office began to show results." "All I need is the office, the rest I will do with my talent."

Jenkins's influential backer who was unable to support his operetta may have been Edmond Sayag, but other Europeans also backed American black talent, notably those who employed Sam Wooding who left New York in May 1925. Wooding had worked with Vodery in France in 1918. Wooding arrived in Hamburg on May 17, 1925, with Garvin Bushell, New York session musician and associate of Perry Bradford and the Aitken brothers; Thaddeus Drayton and his family; and a South Carolina or Georgia musician named Herb Flemming (a friend of Johnny Dunn). Louis Armstrong had been approached but had just signed up with Fletcher Henderson, whose band was in New York and about to embark on a series of recordings that were of great influence on black and white jazz dance musicians in America.[9] Jenkins's friend Evelyn Dove joined them from London. Ellington had assisted with the music. The show was called *Chocolate Kiddies*.[10] They toured Germany and Scandinavia for seven months, also traveling to Prague, Budapest, and Vienna in 1925, and Spain, France, Switzerland, and Russia (playing before Stalin, according to Drayton) in 1926.[11]

Jenkins worked on his art music, achieving some success in July 1925 when his *Charlestonia* was performed at the Kursaal in Ostende. The concert was announced on June 29, 1925, in the Paris edition of the *New York Herald*—a paper selling mainly to Americans in France—under the headline "American Negro Writes Rhapsody." It told its readers "The first symphonic work by an American negro will be heard in concert, it was announced yesterday, next Sunday at the Kurseel [sic] in Ostend, under the conductorship of M. Rasse." Jenkins, the paper told its readers, was the director of music at l'Ermitage in the Bois de Boulogne in Paris.

The Belgian jazz researcher Robert Pernet has traced two reviews of *Charlestonia*. The Ostende newspaper merely said "A Negro Folk Rhapsody was placed in the evening program and achieved a great triumph, which was its first performance. The composer, Mr. Jenkins, was loudly applauded."[12]

The French arts and entertainment magazine *Comedia* of Paris reported in more detail:

> An unprecedented success was achieved at the Kursaal in Ostende by the fautless performance, with the Kursaal orchestra directed by the master, F. Rasse, of the Negro folk rhapsody *Charlestonia*. The composer, Mr. Edmund T. Jenkins, a Negro and an Associate of the Royal Academy of Music in London, attended this concert and was the subject of appreciation by the audience. The famous rhapsody of Mr. Jenkins was put in the program at the special request of Mr. Sayag, the hard-working and far-sighted director of the Kursaal.[13]

Jenkins told friends in Europe and America of this event, and it seems that Alain Locke was in the concert hall that evening, for in 1936 he wrote that Jenkins had broken with the romantic school of music centered on Dvořák and had joined the realistic school of music, writing a black music based on folk jazz.[14] In America in late 1926 *Charlestonia* was described as "a syncopated symphony built largely on Negro themes."[15]

The performance of his rhapsody in Belgium in July 1925 seems to have encouraged Jenkins to write to Gwendolyn Bennett of *Opportunity*. Two pages of the November 1925 issue are about Jenkins, who must have supplied the photograph and a copy of the Ostende concert program. Bennett quoted from Jenkins's cutting letter, which seems to be the source for the remark about the dollar talking previously quoted. Bennett, many years later, was to receive a Pulitzer Prize, but her article seems to be a mixture of information direct from Jenkins, from another source who may be Alain Locke, from her recollection of his visits to the magazine's offices in the winter of 1923/1924, and from the concert program. There are several interesting details of Jenkins's rhapsody. Bennett described the atmosphere at the Kursaal:

> All of a sudden there is a hush and there is something decided in the bow which the conductor makes to the lodge nearest the orchestra. Your curiousity being piqued, you would look at your programme and find there the eighth number. . . . *Charlestonia: rapsodie populaire negre (1st execution)*. One knows that in the music world the first execution of a symphony is a great event to the composer thereof as well as the music world at large. Looking at the program [sic] again we see that Edmund T. Jenkins is the composer. And *mirable dictu*, he is a Negro.[16]

Bennett's article also mentions other works by Jenkins. She wrote that *Charlestonia:*

> was written four years ago while Mr. Jenkins was in London. The work is built on Negro Folk melodies with one in particular being stressed, giving the reason for its being called *Charlestonia*. "Brer Rabbit, what do you do dere" is a tune well known to Charlestonians as that sung by the fishermen on the wharfs. Mr. Jenkins says simply "Remembering the tune from my childhood I was inspired to use it as the theme for my first rhapsodie."

Wendell Bruce James had failed to identify the first theme of Jenkins's rhapsody at the December 1919 Coterie of Friends concert:

the same *Folk Rhapsody* was suggested to Lattimore in the proposed concert for the Pan-African Congress in London in November 1923: Bennett's conversation with Jenkins was in the winter of 1923–1924, and the "four years ago" would fit the proposal that the Kursaal concert of July 1925 was not the premier performance, but that it had been given to the black and white Londoners in the Wigmore Hall in December 1919. Jenkins had retitled his rhapsody, for James P. Johnson's *Charleston* was becoming the dance rage and his home town was to be known by name to millions around the world.

Bennett noted that Jenkins had written a *Rhapsodie Spirituelle* also entitled *Negro Folk Rhapsody Number Two*, which had been completed in the "last two years. Mr. Jenkins says of this more recent work 'I did most of my orchestral scoring of the work while spending the Christmas before last in Charleston.' "

Jenkins's frustrations in America were explained by Bennett, who was able to show that his decision to move back to Europe was a wise one. Not only had his rhapsody been performed, but Jenkins was also operating a music publishing company, The Anglo-Continental-American Music Press at 23 rue Pasquier, the same street in central Paris he had known two years before. "It is characterized as 'A firm to publish modern, light or serious music of a high-class order as well as ballads, popular songs, foxtrots and, in fine [*sic*], a complete line of dance music.' " The business had been operating since at least September 1925.[17]

Jenkins seems to have written a detailed letter to Bennett, for the above quotation, and the following, sound like Edmund Jenkins: "So far these numbers have been published *Rhapsodie Spirituelle*, three art songs with words by Lady Lindsay and the music by Mr. Jenkins—*Doubting, A Romance, The Fiddlers Fiddle; Prelude Religieux* by Mr. Jenkins; and *Romance for the Violin*." The first item was the result of Edmund's stay in Charleston in Christmas 1923 and all the others were works from his earlier days at the Royal Academy of Music. There were also four dance numbers *That Place Called Italy, I Want You Near Me, Amber Eyes,* and *If I Were to Tell You I Love You*.

Opportunity added its weight to the Harlem Renaissance by sponsoring literary contests, and in October 1925 it printed details of the annual contest, with one thousand dollars in prize money donated by Casper Holstein (part Spanish and part black and a gambler, according to Willie "The Lion" Smith), which included three for musical composition, worth seventy-five, fifty, and twenty-five dollars. Works had to be unpublished and were to be received between October 1, 1925, and January 31, 1926. Jenkins sent in two prize-winning items. His *African War Dance* for full orchestra won first prize and his Sonata in A minor for 'Cello won second prize.[18]

On December 12, 1925, Jenkins wrote to his New York friend Des Verney, by now busy with Randolph in the trade union:

> Since writing to you last, I have spent some time in Milan, Italy, and just returned to Paris in time to see Paul Robeson and his wife on their way to South France. I certainly was pleased to have an opportunity of seeing him and personally congratulating him upon his great work.

Robeson had been appearing in London in Eugene O'Neill's *The Emperor Jones* and his artistic success was to lead to years away from America.

Jenkins had been informed by Des Verney that his car was apparently worth thirty dollars, which Jenkins described as "ridiculous beyond words," telling Des Verney to ship the car to him in France, via Le Havre, adding:

> I cannot say that I shall be visiting the States real soon, perhaps in the fall of the coming year; but you may take it from me that I shall certainly keep you informed as to my movements and I solemnly promise you that I will give a true and tried friend as you are ample notice of any intention on my part to visit the States. I won't sneak in, as it were, like I have done before.

Edmund Jenkins seems to have visited Italy at least twice in 1925, as well as the July trip to Belgium from Paris. He was in Paris in November 1925 when he was admitted a member of the French copyright society SACEM (Société des Auteurs, Compositeurs et Editeurs de Musique) on November 13.[19] About fifty unedited works are listed on SACEM's register, from manuscripts returned to Jenkins after their official registration. No copyright fees are noted, and it is doubtful if these works were ever performed after

November 1925 or whatever date they are registered. Jenkins was admitted to full membership on January 29, 1926, and all items are solely in his name except one, *A Prayer*, a song with piano, with the words by "B. Brawley."

A piano work *Spring Fancies* is registered with SACEM, and this might be the piece that Jenkins played on the *Aquitania* on the voyage to Southampton in 1920. The files list *Three Songs (Doubting, The Fiddler's Fiddle*, and *A Romance)*, which had been presented at the Queen's Hall on December 11, 1917. SACEM's references were 299258 to 299260, and the previous number 299257 was allocated to *Prélude Religieux* (the French was corrected, too) which was the organ and orchestra work performed at the Queen's Hall on June 22, 1917.

The four dance numbers mentioned by Bennett in November 1925 were listed—299677 *I Want You Near Me;* 299678 *Amber Eyes;* 299679 *If I Were to Tell You I Love You;* and 299680 was *That Place Called Italy.* An isolated 299725 is the fox trot *The Saxophora Strut.* Dating the entries in SACEM's register is vague; however, a tax of fr12 on *Prélude Religieux* appears to have been paid on February 3, 1926. Sonata in A Minor, reference 300069, had fr24 paid on February 17, 1926. This item won the *Opportunity* second prize announced later in 1926.

If the dates of tax payments and the reference numbers have any meaning, then Jenkins registered *Charlestonia* (300070) and *Rapsodie spirituelle (300071)* in early 1926. In late 1925 he had registered his three act operetta *Afram.* Titles include *Chanson du Prince, Lamentation, Tableau de la Plantation,* a chanson nègre of *O Bye and Bye,* the dance of the cotton pickers, *Nobody Knows de Trouble I see, L'il Liza Jane* and others before the second act, which has the love interest. The work continues with *Blues des contrebandiers et des policiers,* perhaps translating as "Smugglers and Coastguards Blues." The third act has *Beneath the Palmettos and Pines, The Carolina Strut, Kentucky Kate, Pretty Kids,* leading to the prince and princess joining in song, concluding with a *danse d'amour.* This dating is uncertain as entries in the ledger are not in strict numerical sequence and present officials cannot explain the 1926 system.

Rêverie Phantasie for piano and violin has number 302197; *Spring Fancies* (299258) has a francs 9 taxation entry marked "cons.

3.3.26." There is a possibility that a scrap of manuscript survives somewhere in the archives in Paris.

In February 1926 Sam Wooding's *Chocolate Kiddies* arrived in Paris and had two and a half weeks break, and probably joined with Edmund Jenkins, whose office at 23 rue Pasquier was in the music publishing district. The usual gathering place for black entertainers and musicians in Paris throughout the twenties and thirties was the Café Boudon, which was near the Europe district and Montmartre.[20] Jenkins would have renewed his contacts with Evelyn Dove.

On April 20, 1926, Edmund Jenkins wrote a long letter to his father, using the office typewriter and writing from 23, rue Pasquier.

> I trust that this letter will find you well and in a more optimistic frame of mind than that in which you were when last you wrote me. It is very strange to me that you should continue to say to me come back home and all that sort of thing when you know that I have already been back home and tried to find an opening that would be compatible with my life's work and ambition. Since my return to Europe, I have been working very hard trying to get in a position financially to be able to visit you and have you visit me often enough so as to make the distance that lies between us as negligible as possible, just as if I were living in some part of America other than that part in which I was born and which you yourself had admitted it would be impossible for me to live in safety now. Instead of encouraging me in my work, your letters full of lamentations tend to discourage me, and goodness knows with the terrible depreciation of the French currency I have discouragement enough, to say nothing of many of the plans on which I have worked hard thinking that therein would lay my fortune, having all failed realisation so far, and I have to wait and wait simply because I have not the money to back my ideas properly. If I had a little money behind me you would hear of me through out the length and breadth of the country but as I have not I shall have to wait and wait until I get the chance. This chance I am sure I will get in Europe and that is why I look upon it as the only possible place for me to live.

Jenkins explained his wish to buy a small house in suburban Paris "a house with a respectable housekeeper or valet who can cook." "I am tired living in hotels and boarding houses in rented beds and chairs. I want to sit in my own chairs and sleep in a bed that belongs to me along with the other things which give the restfulness of home life."

He asked his father for a loan of one thousand dollars, which, with the franc worth so little, "could get something very nice within a fifteen minutes train ride of Paris."

"I have not been able to get my play produced as yet; however I have composed a new symphony which comprises fifty pages of manuscript and takes from twenty-five to thirty minutes to be played. I have still got to orchestrate it before it can be performed." His letter ended with a promise "to write again real soon."

CHAPTER 21

MOURN THE PASSING

On July 15, 1926, Edmund Jenkins was admitted to the Hôpital Tenon in the eastern part of Paris, where he was to be operated on for appendicitis. Two months later, at a quarter past nine in the evening of Sunday, September 12, 1926, he was dead. The French Republic had ceased recording the cause of death on death certificates in 1912, and official records are not required to be kept after twenty years: the surviving documents in this large hospital show that he died in the Nelatin ward, and that his file was 10392.[1]

Dr. Felix "Harry" Leekam, who was running his own medical practice in London in 1926, suggested that his friend Jenkins had died in great pain, possibly from cancer of the throat.[2] Other folk memories, in Charleston, suggested that Jenkins had slipped in his bath and the complications had led to his death; others said Jenkins had been operated on for appendicitis and was on the mend when he fell out of bed, lay unattended on the hospital floor, and died from pneumonia, weakened by the surgery. If he had been suffering from the tuberculosis that killed most of his brothers and sisters, that combined with the surgery would have kept him in the hospital for eight weeks.

The appendicitis explanation was to appear in the New York *Age*[3] which said "He had been operated on for appendicitis a few days before and had cabled his family in America that he was improving splendidly. Then, without further word, came a cable that the young composer had died."

The hospital authorities registered the death of the thirty-two-year-old bachelor, born in Charleston, living at 27 rue Lécluse, and following the profession of composer. Jenkins had had friends visit him while he was in the hospital, and perhaps they cabled Parson Jenkins. The American consul in Paris cabled Parson Jenkins on September 16, advising that it would cost six hundred dollars to embalm the body and transport it to Charleston. Parson Jenkins cabled Edmund's Paris bank—knowing the address from the loan or loans he had made to help his son establish his publishing business, no doubt—and they wrote back, confirming a cable of the same day, on September 17, 1926.

> We learn that the above died at the Hôpital Tenon, Paris, and that his body was to be transferred to the American Church this afternoon. As regards the sealing of your son's music and personal property, at 27 rue l'Ecluse, we were informed that friends of the deceased who gave the name of Andrews had taken same with the intention of transferring it to 23 rue Pasquier.

Henry Gordon Andrews—"Harry" as Lockhart had called him in 1922—and his wife Nora were in Paris, looking after their deceased friend's affairs.[4] No doubt they attended the funeral service at the American Church in Paris. "In attendance at the funeral were several American friends, including Dr. Alain Locke, Mr. and Mrs. Alfred Renforth Smith, of New York, and their son Albert Smith, the artist, now resident in Paris."[5]

Daniel and Eloise Jenkins advised their friends in America, and the sad news appeared in *The Charleston Messenger* and in the *News and Courier*. The body was shipped on the *Leviathan* to New York, where it was expected to arrive on September 27, 1926.[6] The estate in France was dealt with by an English-speaking lawyer P. G. E. Gide, who listed the items taken from the hospital by the consul, which included Jenkins's passport which had gone to the wrong street in Harlem in September 1924; a walking stick, which may be the one which family legend suggests was a gift of one of the professors at the Royal Academy; $160; a platinum with diamond ring; a yellow metal chain with seed pearls; and a little over nine hundred francs. The consul settled the hospital bill of fr1,376.88 from the cash.[7]

The body arrived in Charleston, and a second funeral was held at the Palmetto Street church on Thursday, September 30, 1926. The pall bearers included orphanage tutors William Leroy Blake and Alonzo J. Mills, and the undertaker E. C. Mickey. The Jenkins Orphan Band and a vocal quartet were present—a final link with the musical origins of Daniel Joseph Jenkins's composer son. Hester Duncan and Julie Fridie sang a duet, and Blake sang one solo, as did Mrs. Ethel Sanford. The funeral ended at the Humane Friendly Cemetery in Charleston, where the body was laid to rest next to that of his mother, Lena James Jenkins. Parson Jenkins insisted on making a hole in the coffin lid, and, removing some padding, was satisfied that the coffin contained all that remained of his last surviving son, and allowed the burial to take place.[8]

The funeral program, kept by the family, is the source of much of the above. It says that Edmund Jenkins was born on April 19, not April 9, 1894, but is correct when it describes him as "Virtuoso, Composer, Conductor."

Benjamin Brawley, at Shaw University at Raleigh, N.C., was unable to attend, but wrote and cabled the family. He wrote an obituary of his pupil, friend, and colleague, which was published in *Opportunity* of December 1926.

> Let us remember this: he not only knew music but at all times insisted on its integrity. For him there was no short cut to excellence. He wanted the classic and he was willing to work for it. He felt, moreover, (and I believe he was right) that there was little creative work in the mere transcribing of Negro melodies. For him it was the business of a composer to compose, and he did so.

Brawley wrote to Mildred Jenkins on September 28, 1926, "I have thought almost constantly of your brother, of our great friendship, and of all that we had hoped and dreamed together." He described Edmund Jenkins as "one of my best friends" and said "my hopes for him were limitless."

Lucien White, the regular music critic of the New York *Age,* wrote on October 23, 1926: "The race has cause to mourn the passing of one of the most promising young race artists since the untimely death of Samuel Coleridge-Taylor, the great Anglo-African composer."

Friends of Daniel Jenkins wrote to him: Mrs. W. J. Howard of

Washington, D.C. wrote "little did I think when you were here telling of his great work that he would be gone so soon." Mrs. Jenkins's sister wrote from Saint Augustine in Florida, regretting "that
all that tender hands may have done for him at home was denied
him." She remembered him as a youth: "I can picture him now, like
Harleston, on the platform of the Orphanage assembly room, playing his first violin solo in public."

Anita Patti Brown, the black opera singer, wrote from Chicago
on September 22, 1926, "What a shock, lately I have thought often
of him. I am planning to go over in December and wanted to write
him if he thought it best for me to come to Paris. Do you think he
was killed. What could have happened?" She asked Parson Jenkins,
"Why did he have to be taken with Paris filled with tramps from
here with no aim in life. Edmund had a task, too sad that he could
not remain with us, until his task had been completed."

Archdeacon E. L. Baskervill, who had spoken at the funeral, was
Archdeacon for Work Among the Negroes, Diocese of South Carolina, and his letter, like many from church ministers, contained a
donation for the orphanage work.

In January 1927 Parson Jenkins received a letter dated January 4,
1927, written by Harold Piper in Trinidad.

> By last mail from the island of Dominica I received informa-
> tion from my friend, Randall Lockhart, of the death in Paris
> of our very dear friend "Jenks." Lockhart and I with your son
> formed a friendship in London in 1917–19 that made us want
> to live for each other; and, I feel, would have caused us each
> to die for each other, if necessary.

Piper had seen the report in Du Bois's *The Crisis*, which may have
been sent to him by Lockhart. Harold Piper told Parson Jenkins

> In this little island of Trinidad there are many unknown to
> you who will share with you your grief. The majority are ex-
> students who knew your son, and in knowing him respected
> him for the fine gentleman that he was—modest, gifted and
> kind. There are yet many others who will feel his loss to us as
> a race, for we all expected great things from him as a musi-
> cian. In fact, what we expected from him can be best expressed
> by quoting from an article I wrote for "West Africa" in Dec.

1919—Mr. Edmund T. Jenkins is a composer who is likely to follow in the footsteps of Coleridge-Taylor.

* * *

In May 1927 Parson Jenkins was informed by a Paris freight company that the *Liberty* was carrying three cases of personal effects on behalf of Mr. Gide and that they would be shipped from New York to Charleston. These cases contained Edmund Jenkins's certificates, medals, musical instruments, papers, music manuscripts, and photographic negatives of black and white friends, two churches in London, the Opéra in Paris, the Queen's Hall in London, and the marching blacks of Charleston's Labor Day Parade.

The music is thought to be with his medals and certificates in a bank vault in Boston, Massachusetts.

* * *

The Jenkins Orphanage is now moribund, having trained over five thousand black waifs. Daniel Jenkins died in 1937. His daughter Mildred died in January 1981. Much of Africa has achieved the ambitions expressed in the 1945 Pan-African Congress. Africa retains its attractions for black Americans, but few are able or willing to go there. Will Marion Cook's son was the U.S. Ambassador to Senegal when Duke Ellington's orchestra toured there. Sidney Bechet died in France. Edmund Jenkins's music is all but forgotten—just as is the music of Frederick Corder and Alexander Mackenzie.

In 1937 Benjamin Brawley wrote *The Negro Genius* and said this of his old friend:

> The music of the Negro and of the world suffered signal loss in the early death of Edmund T. Jenkins of Charleston, South Carolina.[9]

Author's Postscript

While this work was being typeset I traced the widow of Ferdinand Gatty "Ferdie" Leekam, who finally had qualified as a doctor in 1941. On May 4, 1982, I interviewed Mrs. Ferdie Leekam (Miss Marjorie Graham), who advised that she had met her husband at the Iles's home, 24 Goldhurst Terrace. The Graham family lived near this north London street, and Mabs Trollope, whom her husband had first courted, lived in Goldhurst Terrace. Mrs. Iles, the wife of a Port of Spain, Trinidad, taxicab owner and car dealer, was educating their five children in England. The amusing and talented group of mainly black students visiting Mrs. Iles's home impressed her with their intelligence and humanity. She told me that Edmund Jenkins had been a major influence on her husband, whose violin playing pastime dominated his life. He sometimes had played in the dance bands organized by Jenkins. Jenkins's deep religious and musical personality was recalled with fondness: "He was a missionary." Mrs. Leekam welcomed my interest in Edmund Jenkins, expressing the hope that others would be able to hear the music which had so captivated her husband, and which she recalled with an affection almost as deep as her regard for Jenkins himself. She identified the photograph of the Afro-Chinese youth, thought to have been Ferdie Leekam, as another brother, Mac or Mack. Clifford Richardson, a light coloured man, may have been American. She recalled the parties at the Iles's and at the home of Harry and Nora Andrews, and advised that Nora Andrews was English. Harry Andrews was in England after World War II. Dr. James O'Farrell Fletcher had delivered Mrs. Ferdie Leekam's first child, in London in 1934.

In June 1982 I received a letter from Randall Lockhart of Roseau, Dominica. He was responding to three letters I had mailed him in 1981. He too recalled the bohemian parties at Grace Iles's London home, and recalled that the eldest daughter, Ilva Iles, had married Clifford Richardson, and that both had died early, from tuberculosis. (Mrs. Ferdie Leekam had been to one of the funerals.) Mr. Lockhart thought that there was no connection between his London friend and Thomas Lewis Johnson's companion in Africa one hundred years ago. Clifford Richardson, who had a brother also in London, was born about 1898, and had come to Britain in the Trinidad contingent of the army. He was "the archetypal mulatto, the son of a white man and a black woman."

In various letters I had sent Mr. Lockhart from 1979 I had listed various names and sent copies of photographs and documents.

"Ah! That menu of December 1919, most of it I suspect, my handi-work. They used to say: 'Lockie is a damn Frenchman' and then would turn to me for selecting choice dishes and the wines and desserts. The crème à la neige martiniquaise was me harking back to my early days." Remembering events of more than sixty years before, Randall Lockhart, in this letter, described some of the London contacts: "Will Marion Cook, very informal and off-hand . . . Evelyn Dove for whom I had a soft spot . . . I want to but cannot place George Lattimore, Judge McCants Stewart, a fussy but dignified and able little man." He recognized a photograph of Dr. John Alcindor "as someone that I knew well"; he recalled the role in the Aborigines Protection Society played by John Harris; and he also remembered Tony and Jeanette Tuck.

I had asked what his friend Edmund Jenkins had thought of the dance band recordings and life style, which had so concerned Lock-hart and Harold Piper in 1922. "Jenkins felt he had betrayed his artist's conscience when the need of or desire for filthy lucre turned him into a dance band player from his true ambition of creating what we philistines called generically 'classical music.'" This confirms my own thinking when considering the lack of reports in America on his participation in the 1921 recording sessions.

In view of Randall Lockhart's close associations with Jenkins in London, a further Pan-African element, unknown to me, was introduced in Randall Lockhart's June 1982 letter. "The man you call King Amoah III, was he from the Gold Coast and was he by any chance called also Sekyi Touri? If we are thinking of the same man he was one of the most devoted African patriots I have ever met. A handsome and proud man, with a truly regal bearing." This is almost certainly the Gold Coast lawyer W. E. G. Sekyi, a law student in London in 1917 when he published an article in the *African Times and Orient Review*, who was later to reject New World black political institutions for Africa. (See Langley, *Pan-African Movement*, pp. 98-103.)

It is a pleasure and a privilege to be welcomed by veterans who are prepared to share their past; in no instance in my researches into the life and times of Edmund Thornton Jenkins, which were conducted in person or by mail in four continents, have I been refused such cooperation. I hope that this study justifies such confidence and join with Mrs. Ferdie Leekam in wishing that the music of Edmund Jenkins will be performed in public without further delay.

Jeffrey P. Green   July 6, 1982
Crawley, Sussex, England

NOTES

Author's Note: There is no archive of information on Edmund Jenkins or on the Jenkins Orphanage. Original documents are in the author's possession unless otherwise indicated. Interviews were conducted by the author unless otherwise stated. The Royal Academy of Music, London, has some programs of events from 1914 to 1922 and an incomplete set of *The Academite.* Edmund Jenkins's academy details are in the confidential records, and I am very grateful to the Royal Academy of Music for making a photocopy available to me. British newspapers cited are at the British Library, Colindale, London NW9. Postcards of the 1914 band in London are on sale from time to time at London auctions. One has been identified by Dr. Brian Willan in the Plaatje papers at the University of Witwatersrand, Johannesburg, South Africa. The invitation from W. E. B. Du Bois to Jenkins to assist in the 1921 Pan-African Congress in London was brought to my attention by Robert Hill of the Marcus Garvey Papers, Los Angeles, who found it in the Du Bois papers (Reel 9, frame 867). Other information about the 1921 and 1923 Congresses can be found in the Anti-Slavery Papers file G432 at Rhodes House Library, Oxford. Scrapbooks of William Archer Plowright and Mrs. Olive Campbell are privately owned. There is some information on the Congo Institute of Colwyn Bay in the University College of North Wales, Bangor, in both English and Welsh, but this is not complete. The 1921 recordings are not available on microgroove or tape, and I am very grateful to Jim Connor who made his collection available to me, and to Brian Rust who supplied details of the recording sessions and the studio photograph. Karl Gert zur Heide's lifetime of research into black music and interest in the *Southern Syncopated Orchestra* were placed at my disposal, and he also introduced me to Bruce Bastin, whose knowledge of black folk music is voluminous. Karl also told Robert Pernet of Brussels,

Belgium, of my interest, and Robert found the two reviews from 1925. Local newspapers, files of professional societies, the military, and local government all have confirmed remarks made by veterans. Until copies of the *Charleston Messenger* are located, evidence of the activities of the Jenkins orphanage can only be found in the tracts published to solicit alms. Worn and incomplete, there are four in my possession: *God Dealing With Rev. D. J. Jenkins* (undated, ca. 1913); an untitled tract celebrating forty-five years (ca. 1936); *Reverend Daniel J. Jenkins: A Response to Human Need* (ca. 1949); and *History of Jenkins Orphanage Charleston, S.C. 1891–1956* (ca. 1956). Amos White's typescript is in California, privately owned.

1. The Ostracised, Suppressed, and Depressed

1. Census, 1900. 20 Franklin Street, Charleston, S.C.

2. Interviews and telephone conversations, Charleston, 1979, between the author and Arthur Clement, Jr.; Holland Daniels; Sarah Dowling; Edwina Fleming; Lucius Goggins; Inez Nimmons; Emma Reed and Thelma Woods. The ca. 1913 tract *God Dealing With Rev. D. J. Jenkins* has "near Bamberg, S. C., on the second Thursday night in April, 1863."

3. Tract, ca. 1936.

4. *God Dealing* tract, ca. 1913, pp. 10–11.

5. Interviews, Charleston, 1979.

6. Cyril E. Griffith, *The African Dream* (University Park: Pennsylvania State University Press, 1975), pp. 40–57.

7. Richard West, *Back to Africa* (London: Jonathan Cape, 1970), p. 250. Attributed to Edward Wilmot Blyden.

8. *News and Courier*, Charleston, December 13, 1943.

9. *God Dealing* tract, ca. 1913, "Married Sep. 8, 1881."

10. George B. Tindall, *South Carolina Negroes, 1877–1900* (Columbia: University of South Carolina Press, 1952), p. 172.

11. *News and Courier*, Charleston, December 13, 1943.

12. *God Dealing* tract, ca. 1913.

13. C. Vann Woodward, *The Strange Career of Jim Crow*, 2d rev. ed. (New York: Oxford University Press, 1966), p. 40.

14. *God Dealing* tract, ca. 1913. Interviews, Charleston, 1979.

15. Thomas Holt, *Black Over White* (Urbana: University of Illinois Press, 1977), deals with blacks' inability to retain leadership. See pp. 152–153.

16. Tract, ca. 1936.

17. Tract, 1893, South Carolina Historical Society, Charleston.

18. Ibid.

19. *Time Magazine*, August 26, 1935.

20. Tract, ca. 1936.

21. J. B. T. Marsh, *The Story of the Jubilee Singers* (New York: S. W. Green, 1883). Printed at 74-76 Beekman Street. See note 22 below.

22. *God Dealing* tract, ca. 1913, "Damon and Peets, 44 Beekman Street, N.Y."

23. Tract, 1893, South Carolina Historical Society, Charleston.

24. *God Dealing* tract, ca. 1913.

25. Winifred Gregory, *American Newspapers, 1821-1936* (New York: 1937; reprint ed., New York: Kraus, 1967), p. 640.

2. The Impecunious Representatives

1. *God Dealing* tract, ca. 1913.

2. Mrs. Jane McC. B. Wells (Smythe's granddaughter), Triangle, Virginia, letter February 26, 1979, to the author.

3. Willard B. Gatewood, *Black Americans and the White Man's Burden, 1898-1903* (Urbana: University of Illinois Press, 1975), p. 123 refers to the Rev. C. T. Walker, whose biography, *Life of Charles T. Walker* by Silas X. Floyd seems to have been reprinted in New York in 1969. I have been unable to confirm that noted black sociologist Charles S. Johnson was named Charles Spurgeon Johnson after the white preacher who died shortly before Johnson's birth.

4. *The Baptist*, London, September 13, 1895, p. 166.

5. *God Dealing* tract, ca. 1913, "I sent money home from England to cancel all my debts."

6. Dr. Clyde Binfield (Sir George Williams's biographer), Sheffield, England, letter 1980, to the author.

7. London Borough of Bromley, central library, Bromley, Kent, Dunn Collection (a number of photograph albums).

8. Thomas Lewis Johnson, *Twenty-Eight Years a Slave* (Bournemouth: W. Mate & Sons, 1909), p. 107.

9. John Dowling to Martha Stiles, Charleston, 1975; Lucius Goggins to the author, Charleston, 1979.

10. Amos M. White, autobiographical typescript, ca. 1972, which is privately owned in California, confirms the English couple in Charleston.

11. Tract, ca. 1936.

12. John Chilton, *A Jazz Nursery* (London: Bloomsbury Bookshop, 1980), p. 8.

13. Johnson, *Twenty-Eight Years a Slave*, p. 228.

14. *The African Times*, London, 1895-1902; *The Gold Coast Aborigines*, Cape Coast, October 15, 1898; *The Argosy*, Georgetown, British Guiana, March 15, 1902, supplement p. 2; African Training Institute, files EL 359, EL 361, EL 410, University College of North Wales, Bangor. These files include a handwritten copy of the Memorandum of Association of "The African Training Institute 1902," which includes the name of Sir Samuel

Lewis of Sierra Leone; the annual reports 1893–1894, 1908–1909, 1909–1910, 1910–1911, and also 1892–1893. The annual report 1908–1909, p. 21, has "Paul Daniels Charlestown S. Carolina" 28th on the list of students to date.

15. *The African Times*, London, June 1, 1893, p. 91.

16. It had been placed under the foundation stone of the Dart Hall library, King Street, Charleston, and it is preserved in the new building.

17. Lyndesay G. Langwill, *An Index of Musical Wind-Instrument Makers*, 5th ed. (Edinburgh: Langwill, 1977), p. 31.

18. Maud Cuney-Hare, *Negro Musicians and Their Music* (Washington, D.C.: Associated Publishers, 1936), p. 367.

19. Ibid., pp. 353, 368.

20. Tindall, *South Carolina Negroes*, pp. 256–258.

3. He Could Play Any Instrument in the Band

1. White, typescript.

2. Amos M. White, conversation with Richard Hadlock, Oakland, ca. 1975.

3. White, typescript.

4. Ibid.

5. John Dowling to Martha Stiles, Charleston, 1975.

6. Mrs. Sarah Dowling to the author, Charleston, 1979.

7. For details of Mikell's career, see John Chilton, *Who's Who of Jazz* (Philadelphia: Chilton Book Co., 1972), p. 245.

8. *The Journal of Negro History* 2 (1917), p. 257; Holt, *Black Over White*, p. 54.

9. Robert C. Toll, *Blacking Up: The Minstrel Show in Nineteenth-Century America* (New York: Oxford University Press, 1974), p. 249.

10. *God Dealing* tract, ca. 1913.

11. Chilton, *Jazz Nursery*, p. 9.

12. Mrs. Laura Gilbert of Wigan went to the same school as Olive Harleston. Interviewed by the author in 1980, Mrs. Gilbert recollected elders' tales.

13. Mrs. Olive Campbell, New York, to John Chilton, 1979; Miss Edwina Fleming, Charleston, to the author, 1979.

14. *African Training Institute Annual Report 1893–1894* lists Rev. Mr. Packer of Wigan's donations as £3-3s-0d. Bangor EL 361.

15. *God Dealing* tract, ca. 1913.

16. Randall Lockhart, Dominica, letter to the author, August 1979.

17. *The Age*, New York, October 23, 1926.

18. Fred L. Brownlee, *New Day Ascending* (Boston: Pilgrim Press, 1946), p. 135.

19. Margaretta Childs, Archivist of Charleston, letter to the author, 1980.

20. *Opportunity*, New York, December 1926, p. 383.

21. *Morehouse Alumni Quarterly*, vol. I, no. 3, November 1926.

22. *Opportunity*, New York, December 1926, p. 383.

23. Eileen Southern, *The Music of Black Americans* (New York: Norton, 1971), p. 428.

24. Walter C. Allen, *Hendersonia* (Highland Park, N.J.: Allen, 1973), p. 5.

25. Peter Carr, "Leon Scott," *Storyville* 53 (June–July 1974), p. 168.

26. *The Age*, New York, October 23, 1926.

27. T. L. Grant to Daniel Jenkins, September 27, 1926.

28. Willie "The Lion" Smith, *Music on My Mind* (London: MacGibbon and Kee, 1964), p. 97.

29. Summons dated Charleston, October 11, 1920, issued by attorney Frank Frost.

30. Ibid. This clarifies a loan on property near Franklin Street.

31. Amos M. White to Richard Hadlock, Oakland, ca. 1975.

32. Tract, ca. 1930, in the possession of Mrs. Thelma Woods, Charleston. This names Rev. Jenkins's father-in-law as Edward Harleston.

4. The Metropolitan Opera and Prejudice Educate Him

1. Ian Whitcomb, *After the Ball* (London: Allen Lane, 1972), p. 6.

2. See Dena J. Epstein, *Sinful Tunes and Spirituals* (Urbana: University of Illinois Press, 1977).

3. Whitcomb, *After the Ball*, p. 15.

4. Ibid.

5. Toll, *Blacking Up*, p. 273.

6. See Roland Gelatt, *The Fabulous Phonograph, 1877–1977*, 2d rev. ed. (London: Cassell, 1977).

7. Ibid., p. 115.

8. Ibid., pp. 172–174.

9. Bruce Bastin, author of *Crying for the Carolines* (London: Studio Vista, 1971), drew my attention to mail-order credit as a means for obtaining musical instruments.

10. Whitcomb, *After the Ball*, p. 4.

11. See Rudi Blesh and Harriet Janis, *They All Played Ragtime* (New York: Alfred A. Knopf, 1950).

12. *Black Perspective in Music* 6, no. 2 (1978), p. 189.

13. Cuney-Hare, *Negro Musicians*, p. 165.

14. Margaret Just Butcher, *The Negro in American Culture* (New York: Alfred A. Knopf, 1957), p. 67.

15. George Bernard Shaw, *Collected Letters, 1898–1910* (London: Reinhardt, 1972), p. 385. Although Southern, *Music of Black Americans*, p. 297, suggests that *In Dahomey* was a satire on the "back to Africa" movement, *The Times*, London, May 18, 1903, commented "As an example of plotless drama, is perhaps without a rival." This same reviewer added "There may have been an intention to point the contrast between the dignity and picturesque surroundings of the African race in Africa and the absurd aping of white men's ways which is perhaps the most pathetic thing in regard to the "colour problem" of the present day." See *The Era*, London, May 23, 1903, p. 16.

16. James Weldon Johnson, *Along This Way* (New York: Viking Press, 1933), p. 151.

17. Ibid., pp. 209–212.

18. Ibid., p. 215.

19. Eileen Southern, "Frank Johnson of Philadelphia and His Promenade Concerts," *Black Perspective in Music* 5, no. 1 (1977), p. 5.

20. Toll, *Blacking Up*, pp. 216–217.

21. Josephine Wright, "Orpheus Myron McAdoo," *Black Perspective in Music* 4, no. 3 (1976), pp. 320–327. Wright quotes *The Colored American*, Washington, D.C., April 22, 1899, which locates the theater at "Sidney [sic] Australia." See Stafford Allen Warner, *Yardley Warner: The Freedman's Friend* (Didcot, England: Wessex Press, 1957), p. 295. Warner quotes the *Greensboro Daily News*, Greensboro, N.C., June 1, 1941, which states that the theater was "in Melbourne, Australia."

22. Butcher, *Negro in American Culture*, p. 67.

23. Rainer E. Lotz, *Grammophonplatten aus der Ragtime-Ara* (Dortmund, Germany: Harenberg, 1979), pp. 16–17. See Rainer E. Lotz, "Arabella Fields," *Storyville* 89 (June–July 1980), pp. 171–177. Lotz has confirmed that Fields was from Philadelphia.

24. Robert Pernet, "American Negro Minstrels from Alabama," *Storyville* 85 (October–November 1979), p. 30.

25. Rex Harris, *Jazz*, 4th ed. (Harmondsworth: Penguin, 1956), p. 250.

26. Alec Robertson, *Dvořák*, rev. ed. (London: Dent, 1964), p. 67.

27. George Bernard Shaw, *G.B.S. on Music* (Harmondsworth: Penguin, 1962), p. 133.

28. Avril Coleridge-Taylor, *The Heritage of Samuel Coleridge-Taylor* (London: Dennis Dobson, 1979), pp. 26–27.

29. Ibid., pp. 50, 144.

30. Victor 17553 (in the collection of Bruce Bastin).

31. *ASCAP Biographical Dictionary*, 3d ed., 1966, p. 149.

32. Altona Trent Johns, "Henry Hugh Proctor," *Black Perspective in Music* 3, no. 1 (1975), p. 26.

33. Amistad Research Center, Dillard University, New Orleans, La.

34. Program, March 22, 1912.

35. Johns, "Proctor," p. 30.
36. *Opportunity*, New York, December 1926, p. 383.

5. "My Boy Will Have to Leave Very Soon"

1. Donald Knight, *The Great White City* (London: Knight, 1978).
2. Jules Hurtig, New York, to D. J. Jenkins care of the Rev. H. M. Moore, Anderson, S.C., April 14, 1914.
3. Mrs. Laura Gilbert, Wigan, to the author, 1980.
4. Daniel Jenkins, London, to Brooks Brockman, Columbia, S.C., July 25, 1914.
5. Daniel Jenkins, London, to H. Croaxford, London, July 25, 1914.
6. Daniel Jenkins, London, to Lathan, Charleston, S.C., July 25, 1914.
7. *News and Courier*, Charleston, July 31, 1937.
8. James Cameron, *1914* (London: Cassell, 1959), p. 24.
9. Copy in the possession of Mrs. Thelma Woods, Charleston.

6. An Engaging Knowledge of Orchestral Effect

1. Peter J. Pirie, *The English Musical Renaissance* (London: Gollancz, 1979), p. 24.
2. Ibid., p. 37.
3. Ibid., p. 39.
4. Colin Scott-Sutherland, *Arnold Bax* (London: Dent, 1973), p. 10.
5. Ibid.
6. *The Times*, London, August 27, 1932.
7. *Baker's Biographical Dictionary of Musicians*, 5th ed., (New York: Schirmer, 1971), p. 319.
8. Winifred Small, London, to the author, 1979. Other details are from the files of the Royal Academy of Music, London, and from an interview by the author with Mrs. Betty Purcell of Bromley, Kent, in 1980.
9. *Storyville* 78 (August–September 1978), p. 209.
10. Charles Reid, *John Barbirolli* (London: Hamish Hamilton, 1971), p. 26.
11. *Popular Music and Film Song Weekly*, London, October 30, 1937.
12. *Opportunity*, New York, November 1925, pp. 338–339.
13. Frederick Corder, *A History of the Royal Academy of Music, 1822–1922* (London: Corder, 1922), p. 99.
14. *RAM Club Magazine* 49, (November 1916).
15. *Musical News*, London, June 10, 1916, p. 471 (review by J. S. V.).

7. His Effort Was Full of Promise

1. *Whitaker's Almanac*, London 1911, p. 854.
2. Postcard annotated in Edmund Jenkins's hand, "Llandudno 1916."

3. *Llandudno Advertiser*, Llandudno, July 15, 1916.

4. *Who's Who of British Members of Parliament* (Brighton, Sussex: Harvester Press, 1979), vol. 3, 1919–1945, p. 36. Bottomley was one of the few sitting MPs to be arrested. See Alan Hyman, *The Rise and Fall of Horatio Bottomley* (London: Cassell, 1972).

5. Chilton, *Jazz Nursery*, pp. 7–8; *John Bull*, London, December 16 and 23, 1911. John Franklin of Grenada had fathered a child.

6. Ivor Wynne Jones, author of *Llandudno, Queen of the Welsh Resorts* (Cardiff: John Jones, 1975), advised the author in 1981 that Hughes was still an official bankrupt in 1916 when he had returned to Nant-y-Glyn Road.

7. Imanuel Geiss, *The Pan-African Movement* (London: Methuen, 1974), pp. 216–217. Mojola Agbebi (whose non-African name was David Vincent) also attended this Congress, and was an associate of William Hughes. His picture appears on page 10 of the *Annual Report 1908–1909*. His portrait photograph in the archives of the Royal Commonwealth Society, London, was taken by a Colwyn Bay photographer. The *Annual Report 1910–1911*, page 12, mentions Mark C. Hayford. Other west Africans involved with Hughes included Sir Samuel Lewis of Sierra Leone.

8. Corder, *History of the RAM*, p. 98.

9. *Musical News*, London, December 9, 1916, p. 371 (review by J. S. V.).

10. *Musical News*, London, December 23, 1916, p. 471 (review by W. S.).

11. Dennis Plowright (Archer Plowright's grandson), Northwood, Middlesex, interviewed by the author, 1979.

12. William Archer Plowright scrapbook, privately owned by his grandson, Dennis Plowright.

8. The Art of Prize Winning

1. *African Training Institute Annual Report 1909–1910*, p. 3. Scholes is mentioned in the 1893–1894 report, page 7, and his picture appears on page 19.

2. *Wandsworth Borough News*, London, November 14, 1913.

3. Owen Charles Mathurin, *Henry Sylvester Williams* (Westport, Conn.: Greenwood Press, 1976), p. 154.

4. W. F. Elkins, "Hercules and the Society of Peoples of African Origin," *Caribbean Studies* 2, no. 4 (1972), p. 47.

5. Randall Lockhart, Dominica, to the author, August 1979.

6. Information on John Barbour-James has been gathered from *The Argosy*, Guiana, 1898–1902; *The Daily Telegraph*, London, August 5, 1919; *West Africa*, London, 1919–1924; *The Colonial Office List*, London, 1920, p. 666; *The Blue Book*, Accra, 1910; R. N. G. Rowland of Acton,

London; and his sole surviving child, Miss Amy Barbour-James, who also supplied a ca. 1948 extract from *Who's Who in British Guiana*, pp. 632–633.

7. *RAM Club Magazine* 52 (November 1917).

8. Arthur W. Little, *From Harlem to the Rhine* (New York: Covici, 1936).

9. Chris Albertson, liner note to Biograph BLP-12025.

10. Mrs. Sonia Huhn, Bromma, Sweden, letter to the author, March 1980.

11. Mrs. Betty Purcell, Bromley, Kent, interviewed by the author, 1980.

12. *The Academite* no. 5 (Lent term), 1919, p. 113.

13. *Musical News*, London, December 21, 1918, p. 185. The fancy dress dance of November 20, 1918, is mentioned on page 113 of *The Academite* no. 5 (Lent term, 1919). The tennis club plans for the season starting May, 1919, are mentioned on page 107. Lilian Smith was the secretary.

9. The Coterie of Friends

1. Benjamin Brawley, Atlanta, letter to Edmund Jenkins, August 18, 1916.

2. *South Western Star*, London, December 27, 1918.

3. Ibid. See also *West Africa*, London, January through March, 1919.

4. Public Record Office, FO 371/3225, Broadhurst to Balfour, November 15, 1918, "The African Progress Union, an association of Africans from various parts of Africa, the West Indies, British Guiana, Honduras and America." Jenkins was the sole American.

5. Public Record Office, FO 371/3225, Broadhurst cable to Lloyd George, October 16, 1918; FO 371/345, Archer and Broadhurst to Balfour, December 23, 1918; and see note 9 below.

6. *Chiswick Times*, London, December 6, 1918, mentions Archer, Cann, Barbour-James, and Audrey Jeffers supporting a lecture-concert on Tuesday, December 10; ibid., December 20, 1918, reports on the event at Chiswick Town Hall and mentions A. F. Adderley, J. E. Taylor, "and Miss Acham—a young lady of tender age, who was heartily applauded for her song, recitation, and dancing."

7. Amy Barbour-James to the author, London, 1981.

8. *Chiswick Times*, London, December 20, 1918. "The proceeds are to aid the printing fund of a book 'The British African Patriotic Gift Book.' "

9. Public Record Office, FO 371/345, Archer and Broadhurst to Balfour, December 23, 1918. They wanted an African seconded to the British delegation. Broadhurst was of mixed descent, originally from the Gold Coast, according to Amy Barbour-James, who recalled him as a very elderly man in England about 1954, when talking to the author in 1981. Broad-

hurst was in contact with Du Bois in the United States (Geiss, *Pan-African Movement*, p. 235), and with leading figures in west Africa (Jabez Ayodele Langley, *Pan-Africanism and Nationalism in West Africa* (Oxford: Clarendon, 1973, p. 124) at this time.

10. *Opportunity*, New York, November 1925, p. 338.

11. J. C. Smuts, *Jan Christian Smuts* (Cape Town: Cassell, 1952), p. 231.

12. *An Appeal to the Conscience of the Civilized World* (New York: NAACP, February 1920), p. 14. A copy is in the Anti-Slavery Papers, G432, at Rhodes House Library, Oxford.

13. Kenneth Little, *Negroes in Britain*, 2d ed. (London: Routledge & Kegan Paul, 1972), p. 79; Fernando Henriques, *Children of Caliban* (London: Secker and Warburg, 1974), p. 142.

14. *Daily Telegraph*, London, July 1, 1919.

15. *The African World*, London, February 17, 1923, p. 104.

16. *West Africa*, London, August 9, 1919.

17. Little, *Negroes in Britain*, p. 81.

18. *West Africa*, London, August 2, 1919, pp. 639–640.

10. Jazz Comes to Europe

1. *Musical Progress*, London, April 1, 1919, p. 20.

2. George "Ted" Heath, *Listen to My Music* (London: Muller, 1957), p. 28.

3. Harry O. Brunn, *The Story of the Original Dixieland Jazz Band* (Baton Rouge: Louisiana State University Press, 1960), pp. 133–134.

4. Jordan had financed Cook's New York Syncopated Orchestra.

5. *Daily Telegraph*, London, November 3, 1919.

6. Chilton, *Jazz Nursery*, p. 23.

7. Ibid.

8. Olga and Kevin Wright, "My Face is My Fortune—Leslie Thompson," *Storyville* 84 (August–September 1979) p. 225.

9. Southern, *Music of Black Americans*, pp. 362, 369.

10. Randall Lockhart, Dominica, letter to the author, August 1979.

11. *West Africa*, London, August 16, 1919, p. 701.

12. T. D. M. Skota, *The African Yearly Register* (Johannesburg: R. L. Esson, 1932), p. 78.

13. Ibid., p. 272.

14. Geiss, *Pan-African Movement*, pp. 326–331.

15. Dr. Brian Willan's thesis on Sol Plaatje is being expanded into a biography to be published in 1983. He informed me of Xaba's relationship to Plaatje at this time, and also told me about Skota's book (see note 12, above).

16. *African Times and Orient Review*, London, December 1918, p. 98.

17. Ian Duffield, "John Eldred Taylor and West African Opposition to Indirect Rule in Nigeria," *African Affairs* 70, no. 280 (July 1971), p. 252.

18. *West Africa*, London, October 15, 1921, p. 1273. Her marriage to Luke was confirmed by Dr. Felix "Harry" Leekam, in July, 1980, when he was interviewed by Dr. Tony Martin of Wellesley College, Mass. Leekam thought that Luke was from Trinidad. Christopher Fyfe of Edinburgh University, an expert in Sierra Leone history and personalities, informed me that Luke is not an uncommon name in Sierra Leone.

19. William Archer Plowright scrapbook.

20. *West Africa*, London, August 16, 1919, p. 689.

21. *The African World*, London, August 23, 1919. The Coterie had invited James Dossen, Liberian Chief Justice, and Jacob Pieter Crommelin, the Dutchman who represented Liberia in London. (Documents in the possession of the author).

22. *West Africa*, London, August 16, 1919, p. 689.

23. Ibid.

24. John L. Comaroff, ed., *The Boer War Diary of Sol T. Plaatje* (Cape Town: Macmillan, 1973), p. 29. I am indebted to Dr. Brian Willan for bringing this obscure point to my attention.

25. Jabavu's memoir of his father mentions "Mr. I. Bud-Mbelle, who suggested a suitable boarding school in Colwyn Bay, North Wales." Brian Willan informed me of Bud-Mbelle's relation to Plaatje.

26. *West Africa*, London, August 16, 1919, p. 689.

27. Ibid., p. 701.

28. Arthur Briggs, Paris, to Rainer Lotz, April 1980.

29. *Daily Telegraph*, London, August 8, 1919.

30. Ibid., August 11, 1919.

31. Ibid.

32. William L. Patterson, *The Man Who Cried Genocide* (New York: International, 1971), p. 50.

33. Bertrand Demeusy, "The Bertin Depestre Salnave Musical Story," (translated by Howard Rye) *Storyville* 78 (August–September 1978), p. 210.

11. One of the Rising Hopes of His Race

1. *The Clarion*, Cape Town, January 17, 1920.

2. Duffield, "John Eldred Taylor," p. 255.

3. *Daily Herald*, London, December 1, 1919.

4. *The African Sentinel*, London, January 17, 1920.

5. *West Africa*, London, December 6, 1919, p. 1163.

6. Demeusy, "Bertin Depestre Salnave," p. 210.

7. Ibid.

8. Arthur Briggs, Paris, to Rainer Lotz, 1979.

9. Allister Macmillan, *The Red Book of West Africa* (London: 1920; reprint., London: Frank Cass, 1968), p. 195. His business was in Cardiff. Although Randall Lockhart's letters of 1979 and 1981 to the author recalled Manyo Plange with great affection, confirmed that he was the only African in the Coterie, and described his deep love for a West Indian girl in London, they did not confirm that this was the same man. If E. A. Manyo Plange had a son studying in London, it seems likely that the son would be the member of the Coterie. If it was a different Manyo Plange then Edmund Jenkins may have financed the Wigmore Hall concert completely.

10. *African Times and Orient Review*, London, August 1918, p. 16.

11. The files of the Guildhall Library, London, confirm that Harold Piper was a Freeman of the City of London. A photocopy of Piper's application form is in the author's possession.

12. Randall Lockhart, Dominica, to the author, August 1979.

13. Mrs. Mimi Leekam, London, to the author, July 1980.

14. Suits were advertised in the *Times* for £10 at this time.

12. The Lord Mayor Shook His Hand

1. Robert Elkin, *The Queen's Hall, 1893-1941* (London: Rider, 1944).

2. Ibid., p. 19.

3. Dr. Felix "Harry" Leekam, Trinidad, interviewed by Dr. Tony Martin, July 1980.

4. Jack Hylton, "The High Finance of Jazz," *Rhythm*, London, January 1939.

5. Ibid.

6. Edward S. Walker, whose research articles in *Storyville* and publications, especially those with Brian Rust, have shown much of the detail of pre-World War II dance bands, suggested, in a letter to the author, 1979, that drummer Len Hunt had made this remark.

7. Hylton, "High Finance."

8. Dr. Leekam to Tony Martin, Trinidad, July 1980.

9. Randall Lockhart, Dominica, letter to the author, August 1979.

10. MacKinley Helm, *Angel Mo' and Her Son, Roland Hayes* (Boston: Little, Brown, 1942), p. 127.

11. Elkins, "Hercules," p. 53. Some of Hercules's letters from the United States and the Caribbean are in the Anti-Slavery Papers, G432, at Rhodes House Library, Oxford.

12. *The African Telegraph*, London, December 1918, p. 77.

13. *The African Telegraph*, London, December 1919, p. 306.

14. *West Africa*, London, January 25, 1919, p. 902, quotes Adderley's speech, including "Mr. J. C. Smith has told me of Africa; he has made particular reference to the Chiefs of Africa. . . . it left on my mind the spirit that if I belonged to such a race of men I should remain proud." For Smith's biography see Donald Simpson, "Mr. Smith of the Colonial Service," *Library Notes*, new series no. 181 (May 1972), Royal Commonwealth Society, London. Henry Taylor's obituary appears in *West Africa*, London, October 4, 1919, p. 896. Mourners included Frank Lacton, K. F. Tandoh, Robert Broadhurst, John Archer, A. S. Cann, Mitchell of the Coterie with Piper, Audrey Jeffers, E. P. Bruyning, Miss C. Amado Taylor, and Lewis Earl, one of the officials of the club for coloured soldiers and sailors in London's Drury Lane YMCA. Smith's death is noted on page 925 of *West Africa*, October 11, 1919. Dusé Mohammed (or Mohamed) Ali, who had known Samuel Coleridge-Taylor, had edited *The African Times and Orient Review*, and was associated with Garvey. He later was a nationalist in Nigeria, where he died, aged nearly 80, in 1944.

15. Macmillan, *Red Book*, p. 225.

16. David Kimble, *A Political History of Ghana, 1850–1928* (London: Oxford University Press, 1963), p. 545.

17. Macmillan, *Red Book*, p. 109.

18. Leekam to Martin, Trinidad, July 1980.

19. *Opportunity*, New York, November 1925, p. 338.

13. The Remarkable Progress of the Coloured Population

1. Passport Office, Washington, D.C., files "Edmund Thornton Jenkins."

2. *The Academite* 10, p. 200.

3. Program found in Charleston, 1979, in the possession of the author.

4. Public Record Office, BT 27/931; *Imperator*, July 31, 1920, Southampton.

5. Edmund David Cronon, *Black Moses* 2d ed. (Madison: University of Wisconsin Press, 1969), illustration opposite p. 120.

6. Ibid., p. 64.

7. Passport Office, Washington, D.C., files "Edmund Thornton Jenkins."

8. *The Academite* 10, 1921.

9. Ibid.

10. *Opportunity*, New York, December 1926, p. 383.

11. Johns, "Proctor," p. 32.

12. Programs found in Charleston, 1979.

13. Lucius Goggins to the author, Charleston, October 1979.

14. E. C. Lockhart, Fort Smith, Arkansas, to Daniel Jenkins, September 29, 1926.

15. *The Academite* 10, 1921.

14. A Hold on Jazz Idioms

1. Bates had a special and perhaps unique method of instruction, according to Mrs. Betty Purcell, who remembered this from sixty years before, when interviewed by the author in Bromley, Kent, in 1980.

2. *West Africa*, London, November 6, 1920, p. 1426. John Archer of Battersea and Chief Oluwa of Nigeria were there.

3. Amy Barbour-James to Jeffrey Green, London, 1981; *The African World*, London, November 12, 1921, p. 73.

4. Wedding registration files, Brentford, Middlesex, district East Acton, number 257, 1920.

5. Behar, Paris, to Henry, October 6, 1920.

6. Public Record Office, BT 31/32460 "Q S H Syndicate Limited."

7. Heath, *Listen to My Music*, p. 15.

8. Ibid., pp. 28–29.

9. Karl Gert zur Heide, author of *Deep South Piano* (London: Studio Vista, 1970), suggested this date in a conversation with the author.

10. Hylton, "High Finance."

11. Ibid.

12. Ibid.

13. Butcher, *Negro in American Culture*, p. 86. Her book is based on Alain Locke's materials, and thus echoes his comments in *The Negro and His Music*, Washington, D.C.: Associates in Negro Folk Education, 1936, p. 114.

14. The band photograph is from Brian Rust's collection; the sketch is in the Jack Hylton Ltd., London, archives.

15. Postcard, Mimi Durkin to Edmund Jenkins, July 1921.

16. *West Africa*, London, September 3, 1921, pp. 988–994; Langley, *Pan-Africanism*, pp. 70–79; *African World*, London, September 30, 1921, p. xiii. Creighton Thompson is mentioned in Chris Goddard, *Jazz Away from Home* (London: Paddington, 1979), p. 64.

17. *The African Telegraph*, London, May–June 1919, p. 211.

18. *The African World*, London, September 3, 1921, p. 174.

19. Ibid., p. 176.

20. *West Africa*, London, September 3, 1921, p. 988.

21. *The African World*, London, August 6, 1921, p. 28.

22. Edwin W. Smith, *Aggrey of Africa* (London: Student Christian Movement, 1929), p. 57; *African World*, London, July 30, 1921, p. 526.

23. Amy Barbour-James to the author, London, 1981.

24. *The African World*, September 3, 1921, p. 176.

25. John L. Dube, London, to Harris, September 26, 1921, Rhodes House Library G432.

26. *The African World*, London, October 8, 1921, p. 383; the concert was reviewed in *The African World*, October 15, 1921, p. 415.

27. *West Africa*, London, October 29, 1921, p. 1360.

28. *West Africa*, London, November 12, 1921; *African World*, London, November 12, 1921, p. 73. Investigations are not complete on this family, but documents supplied by Robert Hill of the Marcus Garvey Papers, Los Angeles, confirm that Edmund Jenkins, John and Edith Barbour-James, John Alcindor, and Mrs. B. Acham were all committee members of the APU at this time. Victor Barbour-James (1909–1938) cannot be the son reported dead in these two sources; the eldest child, Joseph, a medical student, died aged 22 in 1915. The boy Sendall, named after the governor of British Guiana, seems to be the most likely candidate.

29. *The African World*, London, September 3, 1921, p. 176.

30. *The Age*, New York, October 2, 1926. This was for teaching.

31. Hylton, "High Finance."

32. Hylton, "High Finance." Brian Rust, the British authority on recordings before World War II, suggested May–July 1922 in conversation with the author in 1979.

33. *The Dancing Life*, London, January 1922.

34. Winifred Small to the author, London, 1979.

15. One of the Chic Dancing Places in Paris

1. *New York Herald*, Paris, July 7, 1925.

2. *Opportunity*, New York, November 1925, pp. 338–339.

3. Albert McCarthy, *The Dance Band Era* (London: Spring Books, 1974), p. 12.

4. Ibid., p. 38. Ralton died in South Africa in 1927.

5. Leekam to Martin, Trinidad, July 1980.

6. *West Africa*, London, October 15, 1921, p. 1273.

7. Letter dated "Tuesday" to "Dear Jenks." "When you next hear from me I shall be dying for want of excitement in the little village." Percy Acham-Chen gave his address as Temple House, Saint Vincent Street, Port of Spain. His lawyer father, Eugene Bernard Acham-Chen, the associate of Henry Sylvester Williams, was in China as secretary to Sun Yat-sen. He had been a delegate to the 1919 Paris peace negotiations, and was to be four times Foreign Minister of China. Percy went to China in late 1926 and was advisor to General Motors when they negotiated with the U.S.S.R. He may

be living in Hong Kong at the moment. Dr. Felix Leekam explained the connection in London between his fellow Chinese-Trinidadians and Edmund Jenkins to Dr. Tony Martin in July 1980. Music promoter John Hammond worked with William Patterson in the United States in the 1930s, and Patterson was in Moscow in 1935, when Hammond visited the Soviet Union where he met Sylvia Chen. See John Hammond with Irving Townsend, *John Hammond on Record* (New York: Penguin, 1981), p. 153.

8. *Opportunity*, New York, November 1925, p. 339.

9. Goddard, *Jazz Away from Home*, p. 283.

10. Royal Academy of Music, London, files and programs.

11. Demeusy, "Bertin Depestre Salnave," p. 214.

12. Robert Pernet, "Some Notes on Arthur Briggs," *Storyville* 84 (August–September 1979), p. 206. With Salnave and Briggs in Brussels from September 1924 was Alston "Al" Hughes, a banjo player from Trinidad. Briggs and Hughes were in Turkey before September 1926.

13. Letter to Jenkins, 44 rue de Moscou, from Clovis Brun, 7 Blvd. Rochechouart, Paris, September 20, 1922.

14. Files of the Honourable Society of the Middle Temple, London; letter to the author, 1980.

16. The Very Best Instrumentalist of Any Race

1. *Acton Gazette and Express*, London, February 2, 1923; *West Africa*, London, February 3, 1923, p. 55, and February 10, 1923, p. 88.

2. *West Africa*, London, February 3, 1923, p. 32.

3. *The African World*, London, January 6, 1923, p. 399.

4. *West Africa*, London, April 14, 1923, p. 376.

5. Electoral registers for this street show Howell Buckland and Guy Jones at this address. Information from Richard Bowden, Marylebone Library, London.

6. *The African Telegraph*, London, January–February 1919, p. 111.

7. Macmillan, *Red Book*, p. 109.

8. Leekam to Martin, Trinidad, July 1980. Dr. John Alcindor's son, Frank Alcindor, contacted by the author in late 1981, has confirmed that his father was a keen cricketer, too.

9. Randall Lockhart, Dominica, letter to the author, August 1979. Lockhart recalled traveling to the Caribbean with Major Harold Austin who was an important passenger on the same ship.

17. The Leader of a Jazz-Dance Band

1. Randall Lockhart, Dominica, letter to the author, March 1981.

2. *Diamond Fields Advertiser*, Kimberley, November 14, 1927.

3. *Daily Telegraph*, London, May 12, 1923.

4. Marshall Stearns and Jean Stearns, *Jazz Dance: The Story of American Vernacular Dance* (New York: Macmillan, 1968), p. 135.

5. Ibid., p. 118.

6. Ibid., p. 142.

7. Ibid., p. 144.

8. *Dancing World*, London, August–September 1923.

9. Ibid.

10. Ibid.

11. Companies House, London, file 159946.

12. Receipt found by the author in Charleston, 1979. Dr. Fletcher had a medical practice in London until death ca. 1979.

13. Demeusy, "Bertin Depestre Salnave," p. 210.

14. Shozo and Edith Kato, and their son Hideo Kato, who was serving in the air force, were British subjects on the electoral register. Kato is a name found in Uganda.

15. This is probably Herbert Henry of the Queen's Hall.

16. Sayag at the Kursaal; the Club Daunou in Paris.

17. C. A. Parker for Will Marion Cook, or Moen.

18. Will Vodery? Or possibly Johnny Dunn or James P. Johnson.

18. A Concert for Africa

1. Letterhead in use, November 1923.

2. *West Africa*, London, November 10, 1923, p. 1348.

3. *The African World*, London, November 10, 1923, p. 72.

4. *The African World*, London, November 17, 1923, p. 121; Geiss, *Pan-African Movement*, p. 251; Langley, *Pan-Africanism*, p. 84.

5. *The African World*, London, November 17, 1923, p. 123.

6. Amy Barbour-James suggested to the author, when discussing the events of her school days, that her father had been asked to be personal assistant to Guggisberg when he became governor of the Gold Coast. Barbour-James was a senior postal official in that colony from 1902 to 1917, and Guggisberg, a Canadian engineer officer, worked in the Gold Coast until 1908, making the survey. Kwamina F. Tandoh cabled the news of Aggrey's death from New York to Guggisberg in England, according to Ronald E. Wraith, *Guggisberg* (London: Oxford University Press, 1967), p. 282. Tandoh (King Amoah) attended the 1927 New York Pan-African Congress. Donald Simpson, the Librarian of the Royal Commonwealth Society, London, asked Wraith about Barbour-James on my behalf, but Wraith had no knowledge of the name.

7. Program in the Brian Willan collection. Mary or Marie Lawrence was recollected by Amy Barbour-James in a conversation with the author

in 1981. Mrs. Mimi Leekam recalled that a West Indian "Mr. Drysdale" had taught her singing when she was Miss Mimi Durkin. (Her letter to the author was a direct result of Dr. Tony Martin's interview with her ex-husband, Dr. Leekam, in Trinidad in July, 1980.)

8. Geiss, *Pan-African Movement*, p. 253. The letters to and from John Harris, in the Anti-Slavery Papers G432 at Rhodes House Library, Oxford, indicate just how unbusinesslike Du Bois was in 1921, and in 1923.

9. Document found by the author in Charleston, 1979. Now in the author's possession.

19. A Music School, Publishing Firm, and Orchestra

1. Roland Hayes had recorded in 1918.

2. Tom Lord, *Clarence Williams* (Chigwell: Storyville, 1976), p. 33, repeats the legendary figure of 780,000, but see *Storyville* 83, p. 200. That 258,214 discs of this song sold in one year is a measure of Smith's popularity in black America.

3. Howard Rye, "How Come: Sidney Bechet's Brief Career as Chinese Laundryman/Police Chief," *Storyville* 76 (April-May 1978), p. 139; Chris Albertson, *Bessie* (London: Abacus, 1975), p. 34. Will Vodery directed the show's orchestra.

4. Lord, *Clarence Williams*, p. 515.

5. Mrs. Olive Campbell, New York, to John Chilton, 1979.

6. Laurie Wright, *Mr. Jelly Lord* (Chigwell: Storyville, 1980), p. 20.

7. Stearns and Stearns, *Jazz Dance*, p. 138. See Roi Ottley, *New World A-Coming* (Boston: Houghton Mifflin, 1943), p. 65.

8. Stearns and Stearns, *Jazz Dance*, p. 146.

9. *Opportunity*, New York, November 1925, p. 339.

10. Lord, *Clarence Williams*, p. 81; *The Defender*, Chicago, March 22, 1924.

11. *Opportunity*, New York, December 1926, p. 383.

12. *Opportunity*, New York, November 1925, p. 339.

13. *Opportunity*, New York, December 1926, p. 383.

14. Passport Office, Washington D.C., files "Edmund Thornton Jenkins."

15. William H. Harris, Indiana University, Bloomington, letter to the author, April 18, 1980. See William H. Harris, *Keeping the Faith: A. Philip Randolph, Milton P. Webster, and the Brotherhood of Sleeping Car Porters 1925-1937* (Urbana: University of Illinois Press, 1977), pp. 34-35.

16. Letters from William Des Verney about Edmund Jenkins's affairs are on Brotherhood of Sleeping Car Porters stationery; Edwina Fleming of Charleston suggested in a letter to the author, 1980, that Des Verney and the Jenkins family were related distantly.

20. "I Will Get This Chance in Europe"

1. Karl Gert zur Heide sent me the details of this entry in the Chicago *Defender*, listing the group as Sammie Richardson, Smith, Harvey White, Brassier, Opal Cooper, and Palmer Jones.

2. Stearns and Stearns, *Jazz Dance*, p. 145.

3. Ibid., p. 112.

4. Ibid.

5. *The Defender*, Chicago, June 2, 1923, advertisement reproduced in Max E. Vreede, *Paramount* (London: Storyville, 1971).

6. Paramount 12042.

7. Stearns and Stearns, *Jazz Dance*, p. 289.

8. Société des Auteurs, Compositeurs, et Editeurs de Musique (SACEM), Neuilly-sur-Seine (Paris), France, files "Edmund Thornton Jenkins."

9. Albertson, liner note, Biograph BLP-12025; see also Berhard H. Behncke, "Sam Wooding and the Chocolate Kiddies," *Storyville* 60 (August–September 1975), pp. 214–221; and Art Napoleon, "A Pioneer Looks Back: Sam Wooding 1967," *Storyville* 9 (February–March 1967), pp. 3–8, 37–39. Armstrong had signed a contract to work in New York with Fletcher Henderson.

10. See Behncke, "Sam Wooding," *Storyville* 60; Napoleon, "Sam Wooding," *Storyville* 9 and also Napoleon, "Sam Wooding," *Storyville* 10, pp. 4–8.

11. Stearns and Stearns, *Jazz Dance*, p. 296.

12. *L'Echo d'Ostende*, Ostende, July 8, 1925, p. 1.

13. *Comedia*, Paris, July 18, 1925, p. 2.

14. Locke, *The Negro and His Music*, p. 107.

15. *The Crisis*, New York, November 1926, p. 38.

16. *Opportunity*, New York, November 1925, p. 338.

17. Letterhead dated October 2, 1925, in Mrs. Olive Campbell's scrapbook, privately owned, New York.

18. *Opportunity*, New York, June 1926, p. 189. For details of Casper Holstein, see Ottley, *New World/A-Coming*, p. 65.

19. SACEM, Neuilly-sur-Seine, letters to the author, 1979–1980.

20. Pierre Gazères, Versailles, to the author, Paris, 1979. See Goddard, *Jazz Away from Home*, p. 284.

21. Mourn the Passing

1. Hôpital Tenon, Paris, letter to the author, 1979.

2. Leekam to Martin, Trinidad, July 1980.

3. *The Age*, New York, October 2, 1926.

4. The London electoral registers show that they had moved from 100

Castellain Mansions, Maida Vale, by the spring of 1925.

5. *The Crisis,* New York, November 1926, p. 38.

6. American Express Co., New York, to Rev. D. J. Jenkins, Charleston, September 25, 1926.

7. List dated September 22, 1924 [*sic*]. Daniel Jenkins was still writing to Edmund Jenkins's Paris bank in 1928 regarding musical instruments and other items that had not returned to Charleston. Andrews was dealing with the matter.

8. Lucius Goggins, Charleston, to Jeffrey Green, October 1979.

9. Benjamin G. Brawley, *The Negro Genius* (New York: Dodd, Mead, 1937), p. 299.

SELECTED BIBLIOGRAPHY

Archer, William. *Through Afro-America*. London: Chapman & Hall, 1910.

Bechet, Sidney. *Treat It Gentle*. New York: Hill & Wang, 1960.

Chilton, John. *A Jazz Nursery: The Story of the Jenkins' Orphanage Bands*. London: Bloomsbury Book Shop, 1980.

Geiss, Imanuel. *The Pan-African Movement*. London: Methuen & Co., 1974.

Gelatt, Roland. *The Fabulous Phonograph, 1877-1977*. London: Cassell, 1977.

Hughes, William. *Darkest Africa—And the Way Out*. London: Sampson Low, 1892.

Johnson, Thomas Lewis. *Twenty-Eight Years a Slave; or, The Story of My Life in Three Continents*. Bournemouth, England: W. Mate, 1909.

Pirie, Peter J. *The English Musical Renaissance*. London: Gollancz, 1979.

Ravenal, St. Julien. *Charleston: The Place and the People*. New York: Macmillan, 1906.

Stearns, Marshall, and Jean Stearns. *Jazz Dance: The Story of American Vernacular Dance* (first published as *Dance U.S.A.*). New York: Macmillan, 1968.

Tindall, George Brown. *South Carolina Negroes, 1877-1900*. Columbia: University of South Carolina Press, 1952.

Research articles and rare photographs relating to American jazz music of the style developed before 1940 are to be found in *Storyville* (Storyville Publications Co., 66 Fairview Drive, Chigwell, Essex, England) which started in 1965 and is issued bimonthly. *The Black Perspective in Music* started in 1973 and is now issued twice each year from P.O. Drawer 1, Cambria Heights, New York 11411.

Further Reading

Brian Willan's biographical study of Sol T. Plaatje, which is in preparation at this moment, will throw further light on the black links connecting Africa, England, and the United States in the first quarter of this century. Ivor Wynne Jones is preparing a study of the Rev. William Hughes that will explain the background of Colwyn Bay's Institute.

Goldberg, Isaac. *Tin Pan Alley* (New York: Ungar, 1961), a reprinting of the 1930 edition, details the attempts to link classic European music with folk American jazz.

Huggins, Nathan Irvin. *Harlem Renaissance* (New York: Oxford, 1971) sets the scene in which Alain Locke was a central figure.

Leonard, Neil. *Jazz and the White Americans* (Chicago: University Press, 1962) shows "symphonic jazz" in its era.

Osofsky, Gilbert. *Harlem: The Making of a Ghetto* (New York: Harper and Row, 1965) records the growth of the biggest black city in the world in the 1920s and the massive migrations of southern blacks.

INDEX

INDEX OF WORKS

Opus	Title	Nature	Date	Page
18.	Sonata in A minor for Cello	cello	late 1925	154
19.	A Prayer	song		155
20.	I Want You Near Me	dance	Oct. 1925	155
21.	Amber Eyes	dance	Oct. 1925	155
22.	If I Were to Tell You I Love You	dance	Oct. 1925	155
23.	That Place Called Italy	dance	Oct. 1925	155
24.	Saxophora Strut, The	dance	Oct. 1925	155
25.	Unpublished symphony (this may be the same as Opus 14)		Apr. 1926	157

Note: The lack of information on these, and other possible compositions by Jenkins, is not quite complete. A Prayer was in New York City in the 1950s but is believed to have been lost. The July, 1925, performance of Charlestonia in Belgium was one of at least eight items, suggesting that it was not a lengthy piece. The symphonic work which was scheduled for performance in 1926 may also have been somewhat short, for the orchestra was to be the Pasdeloup Orchestra, a French orchestra usually performing light orchestral works, and unlikely to have given a program centered on Jenkins's work had it been lengthy. If the Jenkins manuscripts are found, it is likely that some will be the student works, and will show the influences on Jenkins of Corder.

The 1921 recordings of Edmund Thornton Jenkins

Note: the number of known versions are in parentheses.

Beautiful Faces	(1)	105, 109
Billy	(2)	100, 103
Bull Frog Patrol	(1)	109
Campañas	(1)	104
Circulation	(1)	108
Coal Black Mammy	(3)	105, 106, 107
Come Along	(1)	109
Counting the Days	(1)	107
Gossiping	(1)	108
Idol of Mine	(1)	97, 99
Ilo (A Voice from Mummyland)	(1)	103
I'm Wondering If It's Love	(1)	99
Laughing Waltz	(1)	108
Love Nest, The	(1)	99
Mon Homme (My Man)	(1)	99

About the Author

Jeffrey P. Green is a writer who specializes in the study of blacks in turn-of-the-century Britain. His outline biography of Dr. John Alcindor is scheduled for publication in 1983, and he is currently researching the life of John Barbour-James. Alcindor and Barbour-James were London friends of Jenkins.

Contributions to the Study of Music and Dance

Music and Musket: Bands and Bandsmen of the American Civil War
Kenneth E. Olson